I0100484

The Real Debate

Our Future at Stake

Biden   Harris   Kennedy Jr   Trump
The Black People's Agenda

WAHIDA CLARK'S
INNOVATIVE PUBLISHING

WCIP Publishing

75 Washington St

PO Box 383

Fairburn, GA 30213

1.866.910.6920

www.wclarkdistribution.com

 www.wclarkpublishing.com

Foreword © 2024 by Wahida Clark

Library of Congress Cataloging-in-Publication Data

The Real Debate: Our Future at Stake

Library of Congress Control Number: 2024946005

Authors: The Black People's Agenda, Donald Trump, Kamala Harris, Robert F. Kennedy Jr., Joe Biden

Foreword by: Wahida Clark

ISBN: 978-1-957954-68-4 (eBook)

ISBN: 978-1-957954-67-7 (Hardcover)

Genres:

• Political Science • African American Non-Fiction • Social Activism

Subjects: 1. Political strategy 2. Black empowerment 3. Voter advocacy 4. Economic policies 5. Social change

Cover Design & Interior Layout by Nuance Art LLC

Proofreading by 21st Street Publishing

Printed in the USA

Foreword

The Real Debate: Our Future At Stake

It is time for Black people, who are often on the bottom rung of economic society, the dying middle class, and the poor to get serious about their future. Which candidate has shown us that they have our backs or best interests at heart 100%? I have not identified anyone yet. This means we must take responsibility and accept the fact that the stake of our future rests with us.

As a Black woman and business owner of WCIP Publishing, founded in a prison cell in 2003, I've always turned nothing into something against all odds. I have navigated challenges and emerged stronger, and I am volunteering to lead this charge. It is crucial that we put our egos aside and mobilize for this life-or-death cause. That first presidential debate 2024, which included President Biden and former President Trump but excluded RFK Jr., was streamed on the X platform. RFK Jr. responded to the same questions as the other candidates. This debate hit me like a lightning bolt, igniting a fire to sound the trumpet and get serious about our future. There is no more time.

Five Action Steps:

1. Form a Strong Team: We need a team of five qualified fact-checkers. This is the first thing we must do—separate the facts from the fiction in all of the candidates' responses.
2. Identify Truth: Objectively evaluate each candidate's statements. Use a simple method:

- Draw a line down the middle of a sheet of paper.
- After research and the fact-checking process, list facts on one side and lies on the other. This documentation will be used to cast our votes, utilizing our voting block.

1. Acknowledge Truths: Recognize truths, regardless of the candidate. If Biden, Trump, or RFK Jr. speak the truth, acknowledge it. We are interested in the facts and whether the candidate is willing to deal with us justly.
2. Unified Voice: Once we identify and acknowledge the truths, we must unite as one voice and form a "Truth Block" to demand candidates address our needs, focusing first on economic independence through policies like Dr. Claude Anderson's "Powernomics."
3. Inclusive Movement: We cannot leave behind the mentally disabled, addicted, homeless, prisoners, and disenfranchised in our collective action.

Together, let's hold candidates accountable and prioritize our communities. The time to act is now. We only have less than 90 days before the election. Is it realistic to put together a 50,000-strong voter block? Absolutely. The Team says we can get 1 million strong.

Join 'The Truth' Voting Block. Identify and acknowledge the truth, be ready to unite, and understand that while we have many needs, our economic situation is a priority. We must all be on one accord, starting with Powernomics.

P.S. When this project was first completed, a historic turn of events took place: a sitting president dropped out of the race, and the Vice President became the front-runner. Since Vice President Kamala Harris attended the Essence Festival, we have included her perspective on administering justice to the Black community, the struggling and dying middle class, the poor, and the disenfranchised.

-Wahida Clark

Open Letter for The Black Peoples Agenda: On the Side of Truth, Seeking Truth Beyond Party Lines

Dear Community,

Are you a Democrat, Republican, or Independent? Red, blue, or white? As Ice-T insightfully noted, "red, blue—they are both wings of the same bird." In alignment with that truth, www.the-blackpeoplesagenda.org website is devoted to facts and realism. Here, you will find articles and videos that aid in seeking factual evidence to make realistic decisions. This movement is not about following the masses, the media, social media or succumbing to hype. It is for those among us who seek nothing but the truth to make informed decisions.

Inclusivity in Our Pursuit

Though named The Black Peoples Agenda, our initiative welcomes everyone who values truth—be they White, Latino, Irish, Jewish, and others who seek transparency and honesty. The mainstream media may be divided into red, white, and blue, each promoting their own agenda. However, our focus remains steadfast on the well-being of Black Americans who have historically been the backbone of the voting system, yet often see little return on their electoral investment.

A Call for Real Change

"Vote for me, and I'll set you free," promises many, yet few deliver. This year, we come together to form a voting bloc, inspired by Dr. Claud Anderson's political action steps #7, #8, #9, #10. It's time for us to demand *Quid Pro Quo*. Which candidates promise to support the Black community in America? They all do. But who will actually deliver? Who will offer us a seat at the table without going behind our backs or hindering our efforts? Our agenda is not to malign any particular candidate; rather, we aim to lay out the facts and make our decisions based on them.

Engagement and Participation

We are on a mission to form a 1 million strong voting bloc. We need volunteers to bring this vision to life and donors to fuel our cause. If you are driven to see real change, join us. Contribute to a movement of truth and justice.

The Voices of The Black People's Agenda

The first voice of our Movement, The Black Peoples Agenda, is Julian Netter. Julian started his journey on the very streets that now challenge our communities. As a returning citizen, he serves as the Executive Director of the nonprofit 'We are The Builders Foundation,' where he has dedicated over a decade to catalyzing the change that Black America urgently needs. His community involvement is extensive, including roles as an Event Organizer for the 'Amendment 4 Passage,' Staff Trainer for State Representative Michelle Raynor's campaign, and Organizer for the 'Florida For All/Win Justice Conservative Ground.' As a Political Strategist, Julian specializes in Resource Connection, Policy Advocacy, Education and Awareness, Community Collaboration, and Program Development.

Join Us in This Crucial Undertaking

We are actively seeking volunteers to fill several key positions within our organization:

- Form a Strong Team: We need a team of five qualified fact-checkers to uphold the integrity of our information. Monique Gamble has already joined us in this vital role, taking point, bringing us one step closer to our goal.

- **The First Voice of The Black People's Agenda:** Julian Netter has taken on this vital role as the face and voice of our movement, ensuring that our message is conveyed clearly and powerfully across various platforms. (3 More Slots Available; 1 more male and two females)

- **Researchers:** To delve deep into candidate policies and actions, providing the factual basis for our advocacy and strategic decisions.

- **Outreach Coordinators:** To manage our communications and event planning, ensuring effective engagement with our community and stakeholders.

-**Data Analysts:** To support our mission with data-driven insights and strategies, helping us navigate complex electoral landscapes.

- **Content Creators:** To develop engaging and informative content that educates and mobilizes our audience.

- **Community Organizers:** To energize and mobilize our voter bloc, facilitating impactful community actions and events.

- **IT Support:** To maintain and secure our online platforms, ensuring the reliability and safety of our digital resources.

- **Publicity Team:** To amplify our message and ensure maximum reach. This team will include:

- **PR Specialists:** To handle media relations and craft compelling narratives around our initiatives.

- **Social Media Managers:** To engage audiences across various social platforms, driving conversation and community involvement.

- Event Publicists: To promote our events, ensuring high visibility and attendance.

We invite you to be part of this transformative journey. Whether you have skills in public relations, social media management, event coordination, data analysis, content creation, or IT, your contribution will be vital to our success. Send resumes, suggestions and ideas: Volunteer@theblackpeoplesagenda.org

Join Us or Donate!

-Wahida Clark

Chief Strategic Officer

The Black People's Agenda Mission Statement

The Black People's Agenda Mission Statement

The Black People's Agenda is dedicated to elevating the Black community by delivering the most accurate and essential information. We are committed to truth and facts, not personal biases, with the goal of educating and empowering our people to achieve wealth, ownership, and control of our own destiny. By addressing the legacies of slavery, we aim to build a future where the Black community can thrive, compete, and reclaim our rightful power in society. Quid Pro Quo: Your vote must be exchanged for tangible commitments to our progress and elevation.

Chapter 1

The Real Debate (Transcript)

BIDEN, Trump, and Kennedy

Speakers:

John Stossel – Moderator, Stossel TV

Dana Bash – Anchor of CNN's inside Politics and co-anchor of State of the Union

Jake Tapper – Anchor of CNN's the Lead and co-anchor of State of the Union

(Audience Clapping...)

John STOSSEL: Welcome to the Real Debate. I'm John Stossel, moderator tonight. CNN is hosting its first presidential debate, 2024. But they did not include the independent presidential candidate, Robert F. Kennedy Jr. So, this evening, live from Los Angeles, we're streaming the CNN debate and here I will give Kennedy the same questions that Trump and Biden get.

You'll see the CNN debate, plus Kennedy's answers here. And this is being hosted on Twitter, X we're supposed to call it, and therealdebate.com. But you could say this is the real debate with all the presidential candidates who polled in double digits. Due to the inclusion of Kennedy's answers, this podcast will last a little bit longer. Now, let's go to CNN as they introduce their broadcast.

JAKE TAPPER, CNN MODERATOR: We're live from Georgia, a key battleground state in the race for the White House. In just moments, the current U.S. president will debate the former U.S. president as their party's presumptive nominees, a first, in American history.

We want to welcome our viewers in the United States and around the world to our studios in Atlanta.

This is the CNN Presidential Debate.

DANA BASH, CNN MODERATOR: This debate is being produced by CNN and it's coming to you live on CNN, CNN International, CNN.com, CNN Max, and CNN Espanol.

This is a pivotal moment between President Joe Biden and former president, Donald Trump in their rematch for the nation's highest office. Each will make his case to the American people with just over four months until election day.

Good evening. I'm Dana Bash, anchor of CNN's "Inside Politics" and co-anchor of "State of the Union."

TAPPER: I'm Jake Tapper, anchor of CNN's, "The Lead" and co-anchor of, "State of the Union."

Dana and I will co-moderate this evening. Our job is to facilitate a debate between the two candidates tonight.

Before we introduce them, we want to share the rules of the debate with the audience at home.

Former President Trump will be on the left side of the screen. President Biden will be appearing on the right. A coin toss determined their positions.

Each candidate will have two minutes to answer a question, and one minute each for responses and rebuttals. An additional minute for follow-up, clarification or response is at the moderators' discretion.

BASH: When it's time for a candidate to speak, his microphone will be turned on and his opponent's microphone will be turned off. Should a candidate interrupt when his microphone is muted, he will be difficult to understand for viewers at home.

At the end of the debate, each candidate will get two minutes for closing statements.

There is no studio audience tonight. Pre-written notes, props or contact with campaign staff are not permitted during the debate.

By accepting our invitation to debate, both candidates and their campaigns agreed to accept these rules.

TAPPER: Now, please welcome, the 46th president of the United States, Joe Biden.

JOE BIDEN, PRESIDENT OF THE UNITED STATES: Folks, how are you? Good to be here. Thank you.

TAPPER: And please welcome the 45th president of the United States, Donald Trump.

STOSSEL: And please welcome, Robert Kennedy Jr.

KENNEDY: Thank you.

TAPPER: Gentlemen, thanks so much for being here. Let's begin the debate. And let's start with the issue that voters consistently say is their top concern, the economy.

President Biden, inflation has slowed, but prices remain high. Since you took office, the price of essentials has increased. For example, a basket of groceries that cost $100.00 then, now costs more than $120.00 and typical home prices have jumped more than 30%.

What do you say to voters who feel they are worse off under your presidency than they were under President Trump?

BIDEN: You have to take a look at what I was left when I became president, at what Mr. Trump left me.

We had an economy that was in freefall. The pandemic was so badly handled, many people were dying. All he said was, 'it's not that serious'. Just inject a little bleach into your arm, you'll be all right.

The economy collapsed. There were no jobs. Unemployment rate rose to 15 %. It was terrible.

And so what we had to do is try to put things back together again. That's exactly what we began to do. We created 15,000 new jobs. We brought on – in a position where we have 800,000 new manufacturing jobs.

But there's more to be done. There's more to be done. Working class people are still in trouble.

I come from Scranton, Pennsylvania. I come from a household where the kitchen table – if things weren't able to be met during the month that was a problem. Price of eggs, the price of gas, the price of housing, the price of a whole range of things.

That's why I'm working so hard to make sure I deal with those problems. And we're going to make sure that we reduce the price of housing. We're going to make sure we build 2 million new units. We're going to make sure we cap rents, so corporate greed can't take over.

The combination of what I was left, and the corporate greed are the reason why we're in this problem right now.

In addition to that, we're in a situation where if you had – take a look at all that was done in his administration, he didn't do much at all. By the time he left, there's – things had been in chaos. There was literally chaos.

And so, we put things back together. We created, as I said, those jobs. We made sure we had a situation where we now – we brought down the price of prescription drugs, which is a major issue for many people, to $15.00 for – for an insulin shot, as opposed to $400.00. No senior has to pay more than $200.00 for any drug – all the drugs that will include beginning next year.

And the situation is making – and we're going to make that available to everybody, to all Americans. So we're working to bring down the prices around the kitchen table. And that's what we're going to get done.

TAPPER: Thank you. President Trump?

DONALD TRUMP, FORMER PRESIDENT OF THE UNITED STATES AND CURRENT U.S. PRESIDENTIAL CANDIDATE: We had the greatest economy in the history of our country. We had never done so well. Every – everybody was amazed by it. Other countries were copying us.

We got hit with COVID. And when we did, we spent the money necessary so we wouldn't end up in a Great Depression the likes of which we had in 1929. By the time we finished – so we did a great job. We got a lot of credit for the economy, a lot of credit for the military, and no wars and so many other things. Everything was rocking good.

But the thing we never got the credit for, and we should have, is getting us out of that COVID mess. He created mandates; that was a disaster for our country.

But other than that, we had – we had given them back a – a country where the stock market actually was higher than pre-COVID, and nobody thought that was even possible. The only jobs he created are for illegal immigrants and bounceback jobs; they're bounced back from the COVID.

He has not done a good job. He's done a poor job. And inflation is killing our country. It is absolutely killing us.

5

TAPPER: Thank you. President Biden?

BIDEN: Well, look, the greatest economy in the world, he's the only one who thinks that, I think. I don't know anybody else who thinks it was great – that we had the greatest economy in the world.

And, you know, the fact of the matter is that we found ourselves in a situation where his economy – he rewarded the wealthy. He had the largest tax cut in American history, $2 trillion dollars. He raised the deficit larger than any president has in any one term.

He's the only president other than Herbert Hoover who has lost more jobs than he had when he began, since Herbert Hoover. The idea that he did something that was significant.

And the military – you know, when he was president, they were still killing people in Afghanistan. He didn't do anything about that. When he was president, we still found ourselves in a position where you had a notion that we were this safe country. The truth is, I'm the only president this century that doesn't have any – this – this decade – doesn't have any troops dying anywhere in the world, like he did.

TAPPER: President Trump, I want to follow up, if I can.

THE REAL DEBATE STUDIO

STOSSEL: Mr. Kennedy, the question was people feel worse off because of inflation.

KENNEDY: And I want to thank everybody for being here and for this opportunity, and thank you, John. I also want to thank Ellon Musk for live streaming this on X, uhm, CNN made some statements suggesting that I might be, uhm, that he might get sued for the and and I'm very very grateful for the courage that he's shown to protect the freedom of speech in this country.

I wanna just orient us a little bit about why we're here tonight. And I don't want it sound like I'm complaining because I'm, uhm this is not personal issue. This is something that should be very troubling for our country. What happened with this debate.

My uncle, gave the first televised debate in 1960. Ever since then debate has been run by non-partisan organizations. The League of Women Voters until 1988 and, and the debating commission thereafter. And this is the first time that a private corporation owns the debate. And it's troubling because CNN is making tens of millions of dollars from this debate and so they've had an incentive to go ahead conclude with the two presidential candidates who's main purpose was to keep me off this stage.

And again, this is not personal issue, this is something that's important for our democracy because Americans feel like the system is rigged. And this is, this collusion with a corporation, or private corporation in both those campaigns are gonna be pumping in tens or hundreds of millions of dollars in advertising. Oh, it's all a big payoff. This is exactly the kind of merger of state and corporate power. And I'm running in order to oppose and it, Americans can believe the system is rigged against them because it is. And this is an example on how badly rigged it is.

STOSSEL: Mr. Kennedy, we're following the rules here, you're two minutes are up. It's your show you should get an introduction like that.

KENNEDY: I got a follow-up.

STOSSEL: We're going back to the debate.

KENNEDY: I got to respond right?

STOSSEL: Uhm, not according to the whoop. Person in my ear here.

KENNEDY: (Laughing)

CNN STUDIO

TRUMP: Am I allowed to respond to him?

TAPPER: Well, I'm going to ask you a follow-up. You can do whatever you want with the minute that we give you,

I want to follow up. You want to impose a 10% tariff on all goods coming into the U.S. How will you ensure that that doesn't drive prices even higher?

TRUMP: Not going to drive them higher it's just going to cause countries that have been ripping us off for years, like China and many others, in all fairness to China – it's going to just force them to pay us a lot of money, reduce our deficit tremendously, and give us a lot of power for other things.

But he – he (referring to Joe Biden) made a statement. The only thing he was right about is I gave you the largest tax cut in history. I also gave you the largest regulation cut in history. That's why we had all the jobs. And the jobs went down and then they bounced back and he's taking credit for bounceback jobs. You can't do that.

He also said he inherited 9% inflation. No, he inherited almost no inflation, and it stayed that way for fourteen months. And then it blew up under his leadership, because they spent money like a bunch of people that didn't know what they were doing. And they don't know what they were doing. It was the worst – probably the worst administration in history. There's never been.

And as far as Afghanistan is concerned, I was getting out of Afghanistan, but we were getting out with dignity, with strength, with power. He got out, it was the most embarrassing day in the history of our country's life.

The Real Debate Studio

STOSSEL: He says the question was prices are higher because of Trump's 10% Tariffs.

KENNEDY: And this is a uh, this is another example of why this debate is the problem because these two men are the people who ran up of the deficit that is causing the inflation. President Trump came into office promising to balance the budget instead, he spent more money in office of every president in the United States history combined. From George Washington to George W. Bush, 283 years of history. President Biden, is, will beat him he's already run up 6.3 trillion dollars in debt and by the end, by time he (Joe Boden) leaves office, he'll run up more than President Trump. That's why we have inflation.

Inflation is caused, because they're printing money to pay for these expenses that we don't have and that money then a tax on the poor, that's why we have a 22% hike in home insurance. That's why we have $4.00 milk, $4.00 bread, $6.00 gasoline, is because of the forever wars and out of control spendings by these two gentlemen. If a $34 trillion dollar debt now, the interest alone is costing us more than our military budget. Within 5 years, .50 cents at every dollar we collect in taxes will go to servicing the debt within ten years, a hundred percent.

This is existential. This is one of the problems that neither of these two will talk about. This is the reason, that they need me on stage, cause I would confront them with what they did. They were the ones who ran up half of this deficit attributable to those 2 men and that's what is causing inflation. We'll never deal with inflation if we don't deal with the money printing problem. And neither of them are gonna do it.

STOSSEL: Money printing. Back to the debate.

CNN STUDIO

TAPPER: President Trump, over the last eight years, under both of your administrations, the national debt soared to record highs. And according to a new non-partisan analysis, President Trump, your administration approved $8.4 trillion in new debt. While so far, President Biden, you've approved $4.3 trillion in new debt.

So former President Trump, many of the tax cuts that you signed into law are set to expire next year. You want to extend them and go even further, you say. With the U.S. facing trillion-dollar deficits and record debt, why should top earners and corporations pay even less in taxes than they do now?

TRUMP: Because the tax cuts spurred the greatest economy that we've ever seen just prior to COVID, and even after COVID. It was so strong that we were able to get through COVID much better than just about any other country. But we spurred – that tax spurred.

Now, when we cut the taxes – as an example, the corporate tax was cut down to 21% from 39%, plus beyond that – we took in more revenue with much less tax and companies were bringing back trillions of dollars back into our country.

The country was going like never before. And we were ready to start paying down debt. We were ready to start using the liquid gold right under our feet, the oil and gas right under our feet. We were going to have something that nobody else has had.

We got hit with COVID. We did a lot to fix it. I gave him an unbelievable situation, with all of the therapeutics and all of the things that we came up with. We – we gave him something great.

Remember, more people died under his administration, even though we had largely fixed it. More people died under his administration than our administration, and we were right in the middle of it. Something which a lot of people don't like to talk about, but he had far more people dying in his adminis-tration.

He did the mandate, which is a disaster. Mandating it. The vaccine went out. He did a mandate on the vaccine, which is the thing that people most objected to about the vaccine. And he did a very poor job, just a very poor job.

And I will tell you, not only poor there, but throughout the entire world, we're no longer respected as a country. They don't respect our leadership. They don't respect the United States anymore.

We're like a third world nation. Between weaponization of his election, trying to go after his political opponent, all of the things he's done, we've become like a third world nation. And it's a shame, the damage he's done to our country.

And I'd love to ask him, and will, why he allowed millions of people to come in here from prisons, jails and mental institutions to come into our country and destroy our country.

TAPPER: President Trump, we will get to immigration later in this block.

President Biden, I want to give you an opportunity to respond to this question about the national debt.

BIDEN: He had the largest national debt of any president in a four-year period, number one.

Number two, he got $2 trillion tax cut, benefited the very wealthy.

What I'm going to do is fix the taxes.

For example, we have a thousand trillionaires in America – I mean, billionaires in America. And what's happening? They're in a situation where they, in fact, pay 8.2% in taxes. If they just paid 24% or 25%, either one of those numbers, they'd raised $500 million – billion dollars, I should say, in a 10-year period.

We'd be able to right – wipe out his debt. We'd be able to help make sure that – all those things we need to do, childcare, elder care, making sure that we continue to strengthen our healthcare system, making sure that we're able to make every single solitary person eligible for what I've been able to do with the COVID – excuse me, with dealing with everything we have to do with.

Look, if – we finally beat Medicare.

TAPPER: Thank you, President Biden. President Trump?

TRUMP: Well, he's right, he did beat Medicare. He beat it to death. And he's destroying Medicare, because all of these people are coming in, they're putting them on Medicare, they're putting them on Social Security. They're going to destroy Social Security.

This man is going to single-handedly destroy Social Security. These millions and millions of people coming in, they're trying to put them on Social Security. He will wipe out Social Security. He will wipe out Medicare. So he was right in the way he finished that sentence, and it's a shame.

What's happened to our country in the last four years is not to be believed. Foreign countries – I'm friends with a lot of people. They cannot believe what happened to the United States of America. We're no longer respected. They don't like us. We give them everything they want, and they – they think we're stupid. They think we're very stupid people.

What we're doing for other countries, and they do nothing for us. What this man has done is absolutely criminal.

TAPPER: Thank you, President Trump.

Dana?

The Real Debate Studio

STOSSEL: Mr. Kennedy, they gave the same question. Before they veered off, the question was taxes. Trump says, lower taxes more stimulus. Biden says, higher taxes more money coming.

12

KENNEDY: President Trump is, I think right. He did have a strong economy. But anybody can have a strong economy by borrowing $8 trillion dollars because you're forcing our children to pay for our present-day prosperity with this enormous debt which ultimately is paid by, paid by the poor, by people with fixed incomes.

I wanna address the area that they veered into which is COVID management. This another illustration by why this is so problematical because these two presidents shut down every business in our country, 3.3 million businesses with no due process, no just compensation. 41% Black owned businesses that they closed will never reopen. There was no scientific reason to do this. There was no public hearings. They were, they made a bad mistake and that was, the worst financial mistake in American history.

They shifted $4.3 trillion dollars upward to this new oligarchy billionaires that he was talking about. They created a billionaire a day, in 500 days. And one of the problems is that CNN was their biggest cheerleader. Oh and the same company 'Blackrock'. (audience clapping) The same company the biggest shareholders, the company that owns CNN or Blackrock and Vanguard those the same company's that own Pfizer. Pfizer's the biggest advertiser. So they were all in cahoots in telling us what we needed to do when we ended up having the worst record of that body count of any country in the world. We had 16% of the COVID test under these two presidents. We only have 4% of world's population. Oh, I don't know why people are getting awards while they were patting each other on the back. We literally, whatever we were doing was wrong. Cause everybody else was doing better than us.

STOSSEL: Two minutes are up. Back to the CNN Questions. (audience clapping)

CNN STUDIO

BASH: This is the first presidential election since the Supreme Court overturned Roe v. Wade. This morning, the court ruled on yet another abortion case, temporarily allowing emergency abortions to continue in Idaho despite that state's restrictive ban.

Former President Trump, you take credit for the decision to overturn Roe v. Wade, which returned the issue of abortion to the states.

TRUMP: Correct.

BASH: However, the federal government still plays a role in whether or not women have access to abortion pills. They're used in about two-thirds of all abortions. As president, would you block abortion medication?

TRUMP: First of all, the Supreme Court just approved the abortion pill. And I agree with their decision to have done that, and I will not block it.

And if you look at this whole question that you're asking, a complex, but not really complex – fifty-one years ago, you had Roe v. Wade, and everybody wanted to get it back to the states, everybody, without exception. Democrats, Republicans, liberals, conservatives, everybody wanted it back. Religious leaders.

And what I did is I put three great Supreme Court justices on the court, and they happened to vote in favor of killing Roe v. Wade and moving it back to the states. This is something that everybody wanted.

Now, ten years ago or so, they started talking about how many weeks and how many of this – getting into other things, but every legal scholar, throughout the world, the most respected, wanted it brought back to the states. I did that.

Now the states are working it out. If you look at Ohio, it was a decision that was – that was an end result that was a little bit more liberal than you would have thought. Kansas I would say the same thing. Texas is different. Florida is different. But they're all making their own decisions right now. And right now, the states control it. That's the vote of the people.

Like Ronald Reagan, I believe in the exceptions. I am a person that believes. And frankly, I think it's important to believe in the exceptions. Some people – you have to follow your heart. Some people don't believe in that. But I believe in the exceptions for rape, incest and the life of the mother. I think it's very important. Some people don't. Follow your heart.

But you have to get elected also and – because that has to do with other things. You got to get elected.

The problem they have is they're radical, because they will take the life of a child in the eighth month, the ninth month, and even after birth – after birth.

If you look at the former governor of Virginia, he was willing to do this. He said, we'll put the baby aside and we'll determine what we do with the baby. Meaning, we'll kill the baby.

What happened is we brought it back to the states and the country is now coming together on this issue. It's been a great thing.

BASH: Thank you. President Biden?

BIDEN: It's been a terrible thing what you've done. The fact is that the vast majority of constitutional scholars supported Roe when it was decided, supported Roe. And I was – that's – this idea that they were all against it is just ridiculous.

And this is the guy who says the states should be able to have it. We're in a state where in six weeks you don't even know whether you're pregnant or not, but you cannot see a doctor, have your – and have him decide on what your circumstances are, whether you need help.

The idea that states are able to do this is a little like saying, we're going to turn civil rights back to the states, let each state have a different rule.

Look, there's so many young women who have been – including a young woman who just was murdered, and he went to the funeral. The idea that she was murdered by – by – by an immigrant coming in and they talk about that.

But here's the deal, there's a lot of young women who are being raped by their – by their in-laws, by their – by their spouses, brothers and sisters, by – just – it's just – it's just ridiculous. And they can do nothing about it. And they try to arrest them when they cross state lines.

BASH: Thank you.

TRUMP: There have been many young women murdered by the same people he allows to come across our border. We have a border that's the most dangerous place anywhere in the world – considered the most dangerous place anywhere in the world. And he opened it up, and these killers are coming into our country, and they are raping and killing women. And it's a terrible thing.

As far as the abortion's concerned, it is now back with the states. The states are voting and in many cases, they – it's, frankly, a very liberal decision. In many cases, it's the opposite.

But they're voting and it's bringing it back to the vote of the people, which is what everybody wanted, including the founders, if they knew about this issue, which frankly they didn't, but they would have – everybody want it brought back.

Ronald Reagan wanted it brought back. He wasn't able to get it.

Everybody wanted it brought back and many presidents had tried to get it back. I was the one to do it.

And again, this gives it the vote of the people. And that's where they wanted it. Every legal scholar wanted it that way.

The Real Debate Studio

STOSSEL: Your position on Roe V. Wade

KENNEDY: My, I have spent probably uhm more energy protecting medical freedom than any other leader in this country. (audience applause) And that, and bodily autonomy, so I think abortion should be the choice of a woman. And I worry about state involvement until their baby reaches viability and I think the states have an increasing viability outside the womb. And I think the states have an increasing interest in protecting that child.

My policy on abortion is called: More choice, fewer abortions. And that's because 52% of the abortions in this country the woman says, that economic considerations were the, were the, played the key role in her decision. Every abortion is a tragedy. Many women don't wanna have abortions over have them because they do not believe they can care for that child for financial reasons. I don't think that that should happen in this country. I have a child, a- a childcare program. As I talked to you before, every dollar that we spend on weapons, provides about two jobs, every million dollars that we spend in that weapons, provides two jobs, creates two jobs. Every dollar, every million dollars that we spend on childcare creates twenty-two jobs. It's good for our economy, it's good for choice, it's good for limiting abortions, and that's why I'll do as president.

CNN STUDIO

BASH: Staying on the topic of abortion, President Biden, seven states – I'll let you do that. This is the same topic.

Seven states have no legal restrictions on how far into a pregnancy a woman can obtain an abortion. Do you support any legal limits on how late a woman should be able to terminate a pregnancy?

BIDEN: I supported Roe v. Wade, which had three trimesters. First time is between a woman and a doctor. Second time is between a doctor and an extreme situation. A third time is between the doctor – I mean, it'd be between the woman and the state.

The idea that the politicians – that the founders wanted the politicians to be the ones making decisions about a woman's health is ridiculous. That's the last – no politician should be making that decision. A doctor should be making those decisions. That's how it should be run. That's what you're going to do.

And if I'm elected, I'm going to restore Roe v. Wade.

TRUMP: So that means he can take the life of the baby in the ninth month and even after birth, because some states, Democrat-run, take it after birth. Again, the governor – former governor of Virginia: put the baby down, then we decide what to do with it.

So he's in – he's willing to, as we say, rip the baby out of the womb in the ninth month and kill the baby.

Nobody wants that to happen. Democrat or Republican, nobody wants it to happen.

BIDEN: He's lying. That is simply not true.

That – Roe v. Wade does not provide for that. That's not the circumstance. Only when the woman's life is in danger, she's going to die, that's the only circumstance in which that can happen.

But we are not for late-term abortion, period, period, period.

TRUMP: Under Roe v. Wade, you have late-term abortion. You can do whatever you want. Depending on the state, you can do whatever you want.

We don't think that's a good thing. We think it's a radical thing. We think the Democrats are the radicals, not the Republicans.

BIDEN: For fifty-one years, that was the law. Fifty-one years, constitutional scholarship said it was the right way to go. Fifty-one years. And it was taken away because this guy put very conservative members on the Supreme Court. He takes credit for taking it away.

What's he going to do? What's he going to do, in fact, if – if the MAGA Republicans – he gets elected, and the MAGA Republicans control the Congress and they pass a universal ban on abortion, period, across the board at six weeks or seven or eight or ten weeks, something very, very conservative? Is he going to sign that bill? I'll veto it. He'll sign it.

BASH: Thank you.

The Real Debate Studio

STOSSEL: To give you the same question, Mr. Kennedy. Should there be any limit on a late term abortion?

KENNEDY: Yeah uh, you know I believe it should be limited, late term should be limited. Absolutely that's what, was permitted under Roe V. Wade. That's what every European country has the same law and that law makes sense, if that baby is fully viable outside the womb, the state has an absolute interest in protecting it. (audience clapping)

CNN STUDIO

TAPPER: Let's turn now to the issue of immigration and border security. President Biden, a record number of migrants have illegally crossed the southern border on your watch, overwhelming border states and overburdening cities such as New York and Chicago, and in some cases causing real safety and security concerns. Given that, why should voters trust you to solve this crisis?

BIDEN: Because we worked very hard to get a bipartisan agreement that not only changed all of that, it made sure that we are in a situation where you had no circumstance where they could come across the border with the number of border police there are now. We significantly increased the number of asylum officers. Significantly – by the way, the Border Patrol endorsed me, endorsed my position.

In addition to that, we found ourselves in a situation where, when he was president, he was taking – separating babies from their mothers, putting them in cages, making sure the families were separated. That's not the right way to go.

What I've done – since I've changed the law, what's happened? I've changed it in a way that now you're in a situation where there are 40%fewer people coming across the border illegally. It's better than when he left office. And I'm going to continue to move until we get the total ban on the – the total initiative relative to what we're going to do with more Border Patrol and more asylum officers.

TAPPER: President Trump?

TRUMP: I really don't know what he said at the end of that sentence. I don't think he knows what he said either.

Look, we had the safest border in the history of our country. The border – all he had to do was leave it. All he had to do was leave it.

He decided to open up our border, open up our country to people that are from prisons, people that are from mental institutions, insane asylum, terrorists. We have the largest number of terrorists coming into our country right now. All terrorists, all over the world – not just in South America, all over the world. They come from the Middle East, everywhere. All over the world, they're pouring in. And this guy, just left it open.

And he didn't need legislation because I didn't have legislation. I said, close the border. We had the safest border in history. In that final couple of months of my presidency, we had, according to Border Patrol – who is great, and, by the way, who endorsed me for president. But I won't say that. But they endorsed me for president.

Brandon, just speak to him.

But, look, we had the safest border in history. Now we have the worst border in history. There's never been anything like it. And people are dying all over the place, including the people that are coming up in caravans.

TAPPER: Thank you, President Trump.

President Biden?

BIDEN: The only terrorist who has done anything crossing the border is one who came along and killed three in his administration, killed – an al-Qaida person in his administration killed three American soldiers, killed three American soldiers. That's the only terrorist that's there.

I'm not saying no terrorist ever got through. But the idea they're emptying their prisons, we're welcoming these people, that's simply not true. There's no data to support what he said.

Once again, he's exaggerating. He's lying.

The Real Debate Studio:

STOSSEL: Mr. Kennedy, what would you do about the border?

KENNEDY: Well, I, I would say on this one, President Trump is more right than President Biden. I think almost everything that President Biden said I know to be, not to be true, including his claim that he was endorsed by the border patrol. Uhm and the, you know the border there's been at least 7 million have come across the border and they've come across principally. And this is without the got-aways which are another 2 million. So those are the people who don't go through the gaps on the wall.

President Biden, when he became the president, ordered a stop on the construction of the wall. Adds the problem. There're twenty-seven gaps in the wall and I stood in Yuma, Arizona, between 2 a.m. and 4 a.m. in the morning. And I watched three hundred people come across. And I interviewed half of them, the first one hundred and ten came from West Africa, young men in military age.

The second one hundred and ten were from uh, uhm Asia, uhm Azerbaijan, from uhm, Nepal, from Tibet, from Bangladesh, most of them were from China. None of them, only two people the entire night, that I interviewed had asylum claims. Only two people, and they were both from Latin... Only people from Latin America, from Colombia and Peru.

I think what President Trump is saying, uh, you know, I don't know how many tourist have come across. I know the border patrol's extremely worried about that. And what's happening is not sustainable. President Biden ordered the uhm, the deconstruction of fences, the censoring, the systems were taken down. I can't tell you why. The long-distance cameras were taken down, the night-lights were taken down. So there was some decision in the administration opened up the border and the two laws that were changed under President Biden as soon... this is the day they came in, the catch and release law. And they legally uhm...

STOSSEL: Time is up, sorry. Back to the CNN Debate.

CNN STUDIO

TAPPER: President Trump, staying on the topic of immigration, you've said that you're going to carry out, "The largest domestic deportation operation in American history,". Does that mean that you will deport every undocumented immigrant in America, including those who have jobs, including those whose spouses are citizens, and including those who have lived here for decades? And if so, how will you do it?

TRUMP: Can I get one second? He said we killed three people. The people we killed are al-Baghdadi and Soleimani, the two greatest terrorists, biggest terrorists anywhere in the world. And it had a huge impact on everything; not just border, on everything.

He's the one that killed people with the bad border, including hundreds of thousands of people dying, and also killing our citizens when they come in. We – we are living right now in a rat's nest. They're killing our people in New York, in California, in every state in the union, because we don't have borders anymore. Every state is now a border.

And because of his ridiculous, insane and very stupid policies, people are coming in and they're killing our citizens at a level that we've never seen. We call it migrant crime. I call it Biden migrant crime.

They're killing our citizens at a level that we've never seen before. And you're reading it like these three incredible young girls over the last few days. One of them, I just spoke to the mother, and we just had the funeral for this girl, twelve years old.

This is horrible what's taken place. What's taken place in our country, we're literally an uncivilized country now.

He doesn't want it to be. He just doesn't know. He opened the borders, nobody's ever seen anything like. And we have to get a lot of these people out and we have to get them out fast, because they're going to destroy our country.

Just take a look at where they're living. They're living in luxury hotels in New York City and other places. Our veterans are on the street, they're dying, because he doesn't care about our veterans. He doesn't care. He doesn't like the military at all. And he doesn't care about our veterans.

Nobody's been worse. I had the highest approval rating for veterans, taking care of the V.A. He has the worst. He's gotten rid of all the things that I approved, choice, that I got through Congress. All of the different things I approved, they abandoned.

We had, by far, the highest, and now it's down in less than half because he's done – all these great things that we did – and I think he did it just because I approved it, which is crazy. But he has killed so many people at our border by allowing…

TAPPER: Thank you, President Trump.

TRUMP: … all of these people to come in.

TAPPER: President Biden…

TRUMP: And it's a very sad day in America.

TAPPER: President Biden, you have the mic.

BIDEN: Every single thing he said is a lie, every single one. For example, veterans are a hell of a lot better off since I passed the PACT Act. One million of them now have insurance, and their families have it – and their families have it. Because what happened, whether was Agent Orange or burn pits, they're all being covered now. And he opposed – his group opposed that.

We're also in a situation where we have great respect for veterans. My – my son spent a year in Iraq living next to one of those burn pits. Came back with stage four glioblastoma.

I was recently in – in – in France for D-Day, and I spoke to all – about those heroes that died. I went to the World War II cemetery – World War I cemetery he refused to go to. He was standing with his four-star general, and he told him – he said, 'I don't want to go in there because they're a bunch of losers and suckers'.

My son was not a loser. He was not a sucker. You're the sucker. You're the loser.

TAPPER: President Trump?

TRUMP: First of all, that was a made-up quote, 'suckers and losers'. They made it up. It was in a third-rate magazine that's failing, like many of these magazines. He made that up. He put it in commercials. We've notified them. We had nineteen people that said I didn't say it.

And think of this, who would say – I'm at a cemetery, or I'm talking about our veterans – because nobody's taken better care – I'm so glad this came up, and he brought it up. There's nobody that's taken better care of our soldiers than I have.

To think that I would, in front of generals and others, say, 'suckers and losers' – we have nineteen people that said it was never said by me. It was made up by him, just like Russia, Russia, Russia was made up, just like the fifty-one intelligence agents are made up, just like the new thing with the sixteen economists are talking.

It's the same thing. Fifty-one intelligence agents said that the laptop was Russia disinformation. It wasn't. That came from his son, Hunter. It wasn't Russia disinformation. He made up the suckers and losers, so he should apologize to me right now.

BIDEN: You had a four-star general stand at your side, who was on your staff, who said you said it, period. That's number one.

And, number two, the idea – the idea that I have to apologize to you for anything along the lines. We've done more for veterans than any president has in American history – American history. And they now – and their family. The only sacred obligation we have as a country is to care for our veterans when they come home, and their families, and equip them when they go to war.

That's what we're doing. That's what the V.A. is doing now. They're doing more for veterans than ever before in our history.

The Real Debate Studio

STOSSEL: Mr. Kennedy the question which neither candidate answered was (audience laughing) there are millions of undocumented immigrants in the country now. What would you do?

KENNEDY: I, I want to comment on their digressions uhm because you know I think President Trump is right that there's a lot of bad people coming in across. I think that's undisputed and we're seeing rise in crime that our associated with the immigrants. But more importantly there's just a sheer number of them and I think a lot of the democrats allowed this to happen out of a humanitarian impulse, out of the impulse of compassion. But when you're actually down there and talking to people, it's not a compassionate solution. The people that I talked to, many of them, they've been extorted, they've been exploited, they've been robbed, they've been raped. Uhm they, they, we have an immigration policy in this country that is now being run by the Sinaloa drug cartel. The border patrol takes because they've been ordered not to do their job, you know, the catch and release. And bring them to the Yuma airport, put them on a plane to any destination they want, this is true. It sounds like hyperbole, but it's not. And they pay their ticket. And if they, if they, and, and, they're, they get uhm, reimbursement from FEMA. It's insane. There's 110 thousand of immigrants now in New York and President Trump's right, they're being put up in a hotel. Many of them are on the street. They have uhm, they have a, they have, asylum court eight, seven years in the future. It can't legally work so they're taken advantage of by predatory employers or paying them $6.00 or $8.00 dollars an hour and there, and those employers are beating against unions shops. Or getting paid $35.00 or $50.00 an hour and the union shops are losing the bid. There are, they are camped out in Randall's Island on the playing fields where children are supposed to be playing for sports. Those fields were closed during COVID, so these kids, these wonderful New York City kids, or scholarship tracks, could not play their sport, and their lives could not, and now they're being, the same thing's happening. They can't play their sports because there's immigrants (inaudible)

STOSSEL: Two minutes are up, sorry. Time is up here. Now three candidates did not answer the question. Back to CNN.

CNN STUDIO

TAPPER: All right. Thank you so much.

BASH: Let's move to the topic of foreign policy. I want to begin with Russia's war against Ukraine, which is now in its third year.

Former President Trump, Russian President Vladimir Putin says he'll only end this war if Russia keeps the Ukrainian territory it has already claimed and Ukraine abandons its bid to join NATO.

Are Putin's terms acceptable to you?

TRUMP: First of all, our veterans and our soldiers can't stand this guy. They can't stand him. They think he's the worst commander in chief, if that's what you call him, that we've ever had. They can't stand him. So let's get that straight.

And they like me more than just about any of them. And that's based on every single bit of information.

As far as Russia and Ukraine, if we had a real president, a president that knew – that was respected by Putin, he would have never – he would have never invaded Ukraine.

A lot of people are dead right now, much more than people know. You know, they talk about numbers. You can double those numbers, maybe triple those numbers. He did nothing to stop it. In fact, I think he encouraged Russia from going in.

I'll tell you what happened, he was so bad with Afghanistan, it was such a horrible embarrassment, most embarrassing moment in the history of our country, that when Putin watched that and he saw the incompetence that he should – he should have fired those generals like I fired the one that you mentioned, and so he's got no love lost. But he should have fired those generals.

No general got fired for the most embarrassing moment in the history of our country, Afghanistan, where we left billions of dollars of equipment behind, we lost thirteen beautiful soldiers, and thirty-eight soldiers were obliterated. And by the way, we left people behind too. We left American citizens behind.

When Putin saw that, he said, you know what? I think we're going to go in and maybe take my – this was his dream. I talked to him about it, his dream. The difference is he never would have invaded Ukraine. Never.

Just like Israel would have never been invaded, in a million years, by Hamas. You know why? Because Iran was broke with me. I wouldn't let anybody do business with them. They ran out of money. They were broke. They had no money for Hamas. They had no money for anything. No money for terror.

That's why you had no terror at all during my administration. This place, the whole world is blowing up under him.

BASH: President Biden?

BIDEN: I've never heard so much malarkey in my whole life. Look, the fact of the matter is that we're in a situation where – let's take the last point first. Iran attacked American troops, killed, caused brain damage for a number of these troops, and he did nothing about it. Recently – when he was president, they attacked. He said they're just having headaches. That's all it is. We didn't do a thing when the attack took place, number one.

Number two, we got over 100,000 Americans and others out of Afghanistan during that airlift.

Number three, we found ourselves in a situation where, if you take a look at what Trump did in Ukraine, he's – this guy told Ukraine – told Trump, do whatever you want. Do whatever you want. And that's exactly what Trump did, to Putin, encouraged him, do whatever you want. And he went in.

And listen to what he said when he went in, he was going to take Kyiv in five days, remember? Because it's part of the old Soviet Union. That's what he wanted to re-establish, Kyiv. And he, in fact, didn't do it at all. He didn't – wasn't able to get it done. And they've lost over – they've lost thousands and thousands of troops, 500,000 troops.

BASH: Thank you.

President Trump...

TRUMP: I never said that.

BASH: ... I'm going to come back to you for one minute. I just want to go back to my original question, which is, are Putin's terms acceptable to you, keeping the territory in Ukraine?

TRUMP: No, they're not acceptable. No, they're not acceptable.

But look, this is a war that never should have started. If we had a leader in this war – he led everybody along. He's given $200 billion now or more to Ukraine. He's given $200 billion. That's a lot of money. I don't think there's ever been anything like it. Every time that Zelenskyy comes to this country, he walks away with $60 billion. He's the greatest salesman ever.

And I'm not knocking him, I'm not knocking anything. I'm only saying, the money that we're spending on this war, and we shouldn't be spending, it should have never happened.

I will have that war settled between Putin and Zelenskyy as president-elect before I take office on January 20th. I'll have that war settled.

People being killed so needlessly, so stupidly, and I will get it settled and I'll get it settled fast, before I take office.

BASH: President Biden, you have a minute.

BIDEN: The fact is that Putin is a war criminal. He's killed thousands and thousands of people. And he has made one thing clear: He wants to re-establish what was part of the Soviet empire. Not just a piece, he wants all of Ukraine. That's what he wants.

And then do you think he'll stop there? Do you think he'll stop when he – if he takes Ukraine? What do you think happens to Poland? What do you think of Belarus? What do you think happens to those NATO countries?

And so, if you want a war, you ought to find out what he's going to do. Because if, in fact, he does what he says and walks away – by the way, all that money we give Ukraine and weapons we make here in the United States. We give them the weapons, not the money at this point. And our NATO allies have produced as much funding for Ukraine as we have. That's why it's – that's why we're strong.

BASH: Thank you.

The Real Debate Studio

STOSSEL: Mr. Kennedy, the original question if anyone remembers it is, it was a good one. It's you say you wanna negotiate with Putin, what if Putin says just let us keep the territory we have, and don't have Ukraine join NATO.

KENNEDY: That is Putin's right now, he's opening bargaining position. Putin has up been asking to settle this war from the beginning. In fact, he agreed to two separate treatise the Minsk Accords in 2019, when Zelenskiy ran in 2019 and ran promising to sign the Minsk Accords. And really the only thing Putin wanted was to keep NATO out of Ukraine. He then in 2022 right after he first invaded was only 40,000 troops. When President Biden said there is absolute baloney. President Putin did not go intro Ukraine intending to conquer Europe. He only sent 40,000 troops. It's a nation of 44 million people. He didn't even want to take Ukraine. He wanted us back at the negotiating table. Zelenskiy asked the United States to help him negotiate a treaty with Putin, and Biden administration said no, who, Zelenskiy then went and asked Israel and Naftali Bennett, the former Prime Minister said yes, and Erdogan in Turkey said yes. And they negotiated a beautiful treaty in Instanbul in April of 2022, they signed the treaty. The one thing that Putin wanted was that he didn't put NATO in Ukraine. He didn't want to conquer Europe and they signed it. Putin was withdrawing his troops leaving Dumba's and Logan's. And what happened? President Joe Biden sent Boris Johnson over to Kiev and forced Zelenskiy to tear up that agreement because they had another agenda which is to weaken Russia.

President Trump was part of it. President Trump gave the first 1.3 billion to Ukraine in 2017 of the first offensive weapons. He then sent Mike Pompeo over there in 2019 to say that we're going to put NATO there. So, and then he walked away from intermediate range nuclear treaty with Russia.

Unilaterally, we had a nuclear weapons treaty that we wouldn't put intermediate missiles in Ukraine or the other former Soviet satellite states and President Trump walked away from it. So, the two of them are equally culpable in the provocations that led to this war. And I'm not excusing Putin. Putin didn't need to go into Ukraine and he should be held responsible too. But we need to look at our responsibility and it falls both on the backs of President Trump and President Biden.

CNN STUDIO

Moving on to the Middle East, in October, Hamas attacked Israel, killing more than a thousand people and taking hundreds of hostages. Among those held and thought to still be alive are five Americans. Israel's response has killed thousands of Palestinians and created a humanitarian crisis in Gaza.

President Biden, you've put forward a proposal to resolve this conflict. But so far, Hamas has not released the remaining hostages and Israel is continuing its military offense in Gaza.

So what additional leverage will you use to get Hamas and Israel to end the war? You have two minutes.

BIDEN: Number one, everyone from the United Nations Security Council straight through to the G7 to the Israelis and Netanyahu himself have endorsed the plan I put forward, endorsed the plan I put forward, which has three stages to it.

The first stage is we trade the hostages for a ceasefire. Second phase is a ceasefire with additional conditions. The third phase is know – the end of the war.

The only one who wants the war to continue is Hamas, number one. They're the only ones standing out. We're still pushing hard – to get them to accept.

In the meantime, what's happened in Israel? We're finally – the only thing I've denied Israel was 2,000-pound bombs. They don't work very well in populated areas. They kill a lot of innocent people. We are providing Israel with all the weapons they need and when they need them.

And by the way, I'm the guy that organized the world against Iran when they had a full-blown kind of ballistic – ballistic missile attack on Israel. No one was hurt. No – one Israeli was accidentally killed. And it stopped. We saved Israel.

We are the biggest producer of support for Israel than anyone in the world. And so, that's – there're two different things.

Hamas cannot be allowed to be continued. We continue to send our experts and our intelligence people to how they can get Hamas like we did Bin Laden. You don't have to do it.

And by the way, they've been greatly weakened, Hamas, greatly weakened. And they should be. They should be eliminated.

But you got to be careful for what you use these certain weapons among population centers.

TRUMP: Just going back to Ukraine for one second, we have an ocean separating us. The European nations together have spent $100 billion, or maybe more than that, less than us. Why doesn't he call them so you got to put up your money like I did with NATO? I got them to put up hundreds of billions of dollars. The secretary general of NATO said Trump did the most incredible job I've ever seen. You wouldn't – they wouldn't have any – they were going out of business. We were spending – almost 100% of the money was – it was paid by us.

He didn't do that. He is getting all – you got to ask these people to put up the money. We're over $100 billion more spent, and it has a bigger impact on them, because of location, because we have an ocean in between. You got to ask them.

As far as Israel and Hamas, Israel's the one that wants to go – he said the only one who wants to keep going is Hamas. Actually, Israel is the one. And you should let them go and let them finish the job.

He doesn't want to do it. He's become like a Palestinian. But they don't like him, because he's a very bad Palestinian. He's a weak one.

BASH: President Biden, you have a minute.

BIDEN: I've never heard so much foolishness. This is a guy who wants to get out of NATO. You're going to stay in NATO or you're going to pull out of NATO?

The idea that we have – our strength lies in our alliances as well. It may be a big ocean, but we're – if we're able to avoid a war in Europe, a major war in Europe. What happens if, in fact, you have Putin continue to go into NATO? We have an Article Five agreement, attack on one is attack on all. You want to start the nuclear war he keeps talking about, go ahead, let Putin go in and control Ukraine and then move on to Poland and other places. See what happens then. He has no idea what the hell he's talking about.

And by the way, I got fifty other nations around the world to support Ukraine, including Japan and South Korea, because they understand that this was – this – this kind of dislocation has a serious threat to the whole world peace. No – no major war in Europe has ever been able to be contained just to Europe.

The Real Debate Studio

STOSSEL: Again, Mr. Kennedy, you may have forgotten the original question, which was as president, what leverage would you use to get Hamas and Israel to end the war?

KENNEDY: Well, I would have used more diplomacy from the beginning. I, you know, I think we have to recognize a couple of things. One is we're a nation of compassion. All of us are heartbroken by seeing the bloodshed that's happening in Gaza. All of us are affected and horrified by the injuries to the civilians in Gaza and the damage to the innocents in Gaza.

We also have to understand that Israel is in the existential battle now and Hamas was a genocidal organization which has pledged to Israel's annihilation, its pledge to the extermination of Jews and it does not want a two-state solution. It wants a one state solution which is Isreal gone, and it actually has in its charter, a provision that says that it is against Islamic Law to even negotiate with Israel.

Oh, Israel is in a five-front war with Hamas, which is a proxy of Iran with the Shiite militias in Iraq and Syria, with Hezbollah, which these are all proxies of Iran in Lebanon. And with the Houthis in Yemen. And it's being attacked on two fronts right now. It is at full war with Hezbollah, and we have to let Israel disarm Hamas. We have to support them. Israel is our oldest ally. It is the only democracy in the Middle East. If you can imagine what a world would be like without Israel for the first time in eighty years, people are entertaining that possibility. And in five or ten years, Israel may not exist because they are no longer dealing with weakened forces that they were in the 2000, 1967 and 1956 etc. Hezbollah is the most proficient guerilla army in the world and probably in history. Iran is now a superpower in the Mid East and has the capacity to maintain a war.

So we need and to wipe out Israel, we need to support Israel but we need to use diplomacy and the people in the White House are not capable of doing that. We need to bring President Xi. We need to bring in President Putin. We even need to be negotiating with Iran and the neocons of the White House. See, this is us as a bipolar world where the United States is dominating the world and won't negotiate with anybody. And that is the problem that caused this.

STOSSEL: Back to CNN.

CNN STUDIO

BASH: President Trump, just to follow up, would you support the creation of an independent Palestinian state in order to achieve peace in the region?

TRUMP: I'd have to see. But before we do that, the problem we have is that we spend all the money. So they kill us on trade. I made great trade deals with the European nations, because if you add them up, they're about the same size economically. Their economy is about the same size as the United States. And they were – no cars. No – they don't want anything that we have. But we're supposed to take their cars, their food, their everything, their agriculture. I changed that.

But the big thing I changed is they don't want to pay. And the only reason that he can play games with NATO is because I got them to put up hundreds of billions of dollars. I said – and he's right about this, I said, no, I'm not going to support NATO if you don't pay. They asked me that question: Would you guard us against Russia? – at a very secret meeting of the twenty-eight states at that time, nations at that time. And they said, no, if you don't pay, I won't do that. And you know what happened? Billions and billions of dollars came flowing in the next day and the next months.

But now, we're in the same position. We're paying everybody's bills.

BASH: Thank you.

The Real Debate Studio

STOSSEL: The question was actually; would you support an independent Palestinian state?

KENNEDY: (Laughing) I'd like to, I'd like to answer the NATO question. I think that...

STOSSEL: You've got two minutes for what you do with it.

KENNEDY: I, you know, NATO, when NATO was created, it was a bulwark against Soviet expansion. President Eisenhower said in 1959, if we do our job with NATO, it will be gone in ten years. And NATO has now become an instrument for the Neocon ideology, which is the, the ideology that is bankrupting our country, it's bankrupt.

We have a huge military budget; we have doubled the military budget that we had in real dollars, and at the height of the Cold War. That money is not being used for self-defense. That money is being used for world domination and to make America the policeman of the world. NATO is the instrument of that. I'm going to, I'm not going to abolish NATO. I'm going to change the function of NATO so that it becomes an instrument of peace and not an instrument of US global domination abroad.

STOSSEL: Would you support an independent Palestinian state?

KENNEDY: I, I, I think that that is, I think that has to be decided between Israel and Palestine.

STOSSEL: Back to CNN.

CNN STUDIO

TAPPER: Let's turn to the issue of democracy. Former President Trump, I want to ask you about January 6, 2021. After you rallied your supporters that day, some of them stormed the Capitol to stop the constitutionally mandated counting of electoral votes. As president, you swore an oath to, , "Preserve, protect and defend," the Constitution. What do you say to voters who believe that you violated that oath through your actions and inaction on January 6th and worry that you'll do it again?

TRUMP: Well, I don't think too many believe that. And let me tell you about January 6th, on January 6th, we had a great border, nobody coming through, very few. On January 6th, we were energy independent. On January 6th, we had the lowest taxes ever, we had the lowest regulations ever. On January 6th, we were respected all over the world.

All over the world we were respected, and then he comes in, and we're now laughed at, we're like a bunch of stupid people. What happened to the United States' reputation under this man's leadership is horrible, including weaponization, which I'm sure at some point you'll be talking about, where he goes after his political opponent because he can't beat him fair and square.

TAPPER: You have eighty seconds left. My question was, What do you say to those voters who believe that you violated your constitutional oath through your actions, inaction on January 6th, 2021, and worry that you'll do it again?

TRUMP: Well, I didn't say that to anybody. I said peacefully and patriotically. And Nancy Pelosi, if you just watch the news from two days ago, on tape to her daughter, who's a documentary filmmaker, as they say, what she's saying, oh, no, it's my responsibility, I was responsible for this. Because I offered her 10,000 soldiers or National Guard, and she turned them down. And the mayor of – in writing, by the way, the mayor. In writing turned it down, the mayor of D.C. They turned it down.

I offered 10,000 because I could see – I had virtually nothing to do. They asked me to go make a speech. I could see what was happening. Everybody was saying they're going to be there on January 6th. They're going to be there. And I said, you know what? There's a lot of people coming, you could feel it. You could feel it too. And you could feel it. And I said, they ought to have some National Guard or whatever. And I offered it to her. And she now admits that she turned it down. And it was the same day. She was – I don't know, you can't be very happy with her daughter because it made her into a liar. She said, 'I take full responsibility for January 6th'.

TAPPER: President Biden?

BIDEN: Look, he encouraged those folks to go up on Capitol Hill, number one. I sat in that dining room off the Oval Office – he sat there for three hours, three hours, watching, begging – being begged by his vice president and a number of his colleagues and Republicans as well to do something, to call for a stop, to end it. Instead, he talked – they've talked about these people being patriots and – and great patrons of America. In fact, he says he'll now forgive them for what they've done. They've been convicted. He says he wants to commute their sentences and say that – no.

He went to every single court in the nation, I don't know how many cases, scores of cases, including the Supreme Court, and they said they said – they said, no, no, this guy, this guy is responsible for doing what is being – was done.

He didn't do a damn thing. And these people should be in jail. And they should be the ones who are being held accountable. And he wants to let them all out.

And now he says if he loses again, such a whiner that he is, that there could be a bloodbath.

TAPPER: Thank you, President Biden. President Trump?

TRUMP: What they've done to some people that are so innocent, you ought to be ashamed of yourself, what you have done, how you've destroyed the lives of so many people. When they ripped down Portland, when they ripped down many other cities – you go to Minnesota, Minneapolis, what they've done there with the fires all over the city. If I didn't bring in the National Guard, that city would have been destroyed.

When you look at all of the – they took over big chunks of Seattle. I was all set to bring in the National Guard. They heard that, they saw them coming and they left immediately. What he said about this whole subject is so off. Peacefully patriotic.

One other thing, the unselect committee, which is basically two horrible Republicans that are all gone now, out of office, and Democrats, all Democrats, they destroyed and deleted all of the information they found, because they found out we were right. We were right. And they deleted and destroyed all of the information.

They should go to jail for that. If a Republican did that, they'd go to jail.

TAPPER: Thank you, President Trump.

President Biden, I want to give you a minute.

BIDEN: The only person on this stage that is a convicted felon is the man I'm looking at right now. And the fact of the matter is, he is – what he's telling you is simply not true.

The fact is that there was no effort on his part to stop what was going on up on Capitol Hill. And all those people, every one of those who were convicted, deserves to be convicted. The idea that they didn't kill somebody, just went in and broke down doors, broke the windows, occupied offices, turned over desks, turned them over, statues – the idea that those people are patriots? Come on.

When I asked him, the first of two debates we had – debates we had the first time around, I said, will you denounce the Proud Boys? He said, no, I'll tell them to stand by. The idea he's refusing – will you denounce these guys? Will you denounce the people we're talking about now? Will you denounce the people who attacked that Capitol? What are you going to do?

The Real Debate Studio

STOSSEL: Well, January 6th obviously doesn't apply to you. But when would you bring in the National Guard?

KENNEDY: Well, let me comment on, on what they were saying. You know, I don't know if, if President Trump obstructed the orderly transition of power which is one of the keystones of American democracy and if he did, he should be punished for it, he should be held accountable. But to me, there's a larger issue which is that both of these presidents swore to uphold and the constitution. They are both wearing American flag pins on their on their vest, on their lapels. That's easy to do. That's an accessory. That's an accouterment. It is a uhm, it's a, it's a, it's a badge of patriotism, a real patriotism means protecting the United States constitution and what they and both of them subverted the right to free speech, and the most important, right?

President Biden, thirty-seven hours after he took the oath of office was ordering social media sites to censor his political opponents. I'm not just talking about me and I'm not just talking about COVID, but I know all kinds of issues like Ukraine, etcetera. This has never happened in American history. He opened a portal, the FBI the CIA CNIH, DHS, the IRS and other agencies to go in and tamper with, with social media sites to take out things that were not politically palatable.

They violated freedom of worship. The two of them are shutting down every church in this country with no scientific citation. They violated freedom of assembly with mass regulations. That again, the top scientists in this country, Anthony Fauci admitted, to Congress two weeks ago that they were not scientifically based. They shut down the Seventh Amendment right to jury trials by saying you couldn't sue somebody who was involved in COVID no matter how negligent that corporation were the biggest corporations in the world, no matter how reckless their behavior, no matter how grievous your injury, you could not sue them.

They shut down 3.3 million businesses with no due process and no just compensation. In violation of the Fifth Amendment. They shut down the Fourth Amendment prohibitions against warrantless searches and seizures with this track and trace surveillance. That was the all out assault on the constitution that we've never seen the likes of that at any time in American History. And I don't believe they have the right to wear those American flag pins. That's it..

STOSSEL: Back to CNN (audience clapping).

CNN STUDIO

TAPPER: I'm going to give you a – a minute, President Trump, for a follow-up question I have.

After a jury convicted you of thirty-four felonies last month, you said if re-elected you would, "Have every legal right to go after," your political opponents. You just talked about members of the Select Committee on January 6th going to jail.

Your main political opponent is standing on stage with you tonight. Can you clarify exactly what it means about you feeling you have every right to go after your political opponents?

TRUMP: Well, I said my retribution is going to be success. We're going to make this country successful again, because right now it's a failing nation. My retribution's going to be success.

But when he talks about a convicted felon, his son is a convicted felon at a very high level. His son is convicted. Going to be convicted probably numerous other times. He should have been convicted before, but his Justice Department let the statute of limitations lapse on the most important things.

But he could be a convicted felon as soon as he gets out of office. Joe could be a convicted felon with all of the things that he's done. He's done horrible things. All of the death caused at the border, telling the Ukrainian people that we're going to want a billion dollars or you change the prosecutor, otherwise, you're not getting a billion dollars.

If I ever said that, that's quid pro quo. That – we're not going to do anything, we're not going to give you a billion dollars unless you change your prosecutor having to do with his son.

This man is a criminal. This man – you're lucky. You're lucky.

I did nothing wrong. We'd have a system that was rigged and disgusting. I did nothing wrong.

TAPPER: Thank you, President Trump. President Biden, you have said – I'm coming right to you, sir. You – well, you want to respond? Go ahead. I'll give you a minute to respond.

BIDEN: The idea that I did anything wrong relative to what you're talking about is outrageous. It's simply a lie, number one.

Number two, the idea that you have a right to seek retribution against any American just because you're a president is wrong, is simply wrong. No president's ever spoken like that before. No president in our history has spoken like that before.

Number three, the crimes that you are still charged with – and think of all the civil penalties you have. How many billions of dollars do you owe in civil penalties for molesting a woman in public, for doing a whole range of things, of having sex with a porn star on the night – and – while your wife was pregnant? I mean, what are you talking about? You have the morals of an alley cat.

TAPPER: Give you a minute, sir.

TRUMP: I didn't have sex with a porn star, number one. Number two, that was a case that was started and moved – they moved a high-ranking official, a DOJ, into the Manhattan D.A.'s office to start that case. That case is going to be appealed in one.

We had a very terrible judge, a horrible judge, Democrat. The prosecutor were all high-ranking Democrats, appointed people. And the – both the civil and the criminal.

He basically went after his political opponent because he thought it was going to damage me. But when the public found out about these cases – because they understand it better than he does, he has no idea what these cases are. But when he – they – when they found out about these cases, you know what they did? My poll numbers went up, way up. You know that because you're reporting it. And we took in more money in the last two weeks than we've ever taken in in the history of any campaign, I don't think any campaign has ever taken.

Hundreds of millions of dollars came pouring in because the public knows it's a scam and it's a guy that's after his political opponent because he can't win fair and square.

TAPPER: Thank you, President Trump.

The Real Debate Studio

STOSSEL: Again, the question doesn't really apply to you. But what do you think about the, the lawsuits against Donald Trump?

KENNEDY: Well, here's what I say, President Biden made the point that it's wrong for a federal official to use political... his federal government, governmental powers is an abuse of power. To use that to punish or disadvantage his political opponents. But President Biden is doing that every day. They've denied me secret service A president... I, I'm the... I'm the first candidate since my father was killed. When my father was killed. Secret service became available to the political candidates prior to the convention, thirty-three political candidates have been given that prior to the 100-day cut off, 120 days, cut off. And most of them with polling number, a tiny fraction of what I have.

Uh President Biden, I am the first candidate since 1968 to request service protection in which it has been denied and that is way of using the federal, of weaponizing the federal agencies to punish a political opponent. I, you know, I think President Trump was right. I am not a fan of President Trump. I'm running against him. I think he was a bad president, but he is right that it's, it's shocking, that fifty-one CIA agents signed this document saying that the Hunter Biden laptop was a Russian hoax when, and they were accusing the Russians of tampering with our election was actually the CIA tampering with the election. I want to say this too.

President Biden is now deployed. You know, he's got $3 billion from big corporations in this country. He's using that corporate money to sue me in virtually every state to keep me off the ballot. That's not democratic. We all, you know, as of a couple of days ago, (applause) let me just finish this. President Biden was criticizing and ridiculing Vladimir Putin. You're getting 88% vote in Russia.

STOSSEL: Mr. Kennedy...

KENNEDY: Let me just finish this point. The way that, Putin got 88% of the vote was by censoring his opponents on state owned television, all the national TV networks and by making sure they didn't get on the ballot. We should not be doing that here in this country. We should be an example of something better.

STOSSEL: I should also add something we are doing that I don't think we should be doing. We said the rules would be the same for you as for them. I've been asking my ear to give you more time, but I don't think that's right. So, I'm going to stop doing that. Back to CNN.

CNN STUDIO

TAPPER: President Biden, you have said, quote, "Donald Trump and his MAGA Republicans are determined to destroy American democracy." Do you believe that the tens of millions of Americans who are likely to vote for President Trump will be voting against American democracy?

BIDEN: The more they know about what he's done, yes. The more they know about what he's done. And there's a lot more coming. He's got a lot of cases around the road coming around. He's got – he's got a whole range of issues he has to face. I don't know what the juries will do, but I do know – I do know he has a real problem.

And so the fact that – could you ever think you're hearing any president say that, 'I'm going to seek retribution?' Do you ever hear any president say that he thought, 'Hitler might've had some good ideas'?

What got me involved to run in the first place after my son had died, I decided – in Iraq – because of Iraq, I said, I wasn't going to run again. Until I saw what happened in Charlottesville, Virginia, people coming out of the woods carrying swastikas on torches – torches and singing the same antisemitic bile they sang when – back in Germany.

And what did – and the young woman got killed. I spoke to the mother. And she – they asked him, they said, what – well, what do you think of those people, the people who – the one who – the ones who tried to stop it and the ones who said, 'I think there's fine people on both sides'.

What American president would ever say Nazis coming out of fields, carrying torches, singing the same antisemitic bile, carrying swastikas, were fine people?

This is a guy who says Hitler's done, 'some good things'. I'd like to know what they are, the good things Hitler's done. That's what he said.

This guy has no sense of American democracy.

TAPPER: President Trump?

TRUMP: Jake, both of you know that story's been totally wiped out. Because when you see the sentence, it said 100% exoneration on there. So he just keeps it going.

He says he ran because of Charlottesville. He didn't run because of Charlottesville. He ran because it was his last chance at – he's not equipped to be president. You know it and I know it.

It's ridiculous. We have a debate. We're trying to justify his presidency.

His presidency, his – without question, the worst president, the worst presidency in the history of our country. We shouldn't be having a debate about it. There's nothing to debate.

He made up the Charlottesville story and you'll see it's debunked all over the place. Every anchor has – every reasonable anchor has debunked it.

And just the other day it came out where it was fully debunked. It's a nonsense story. He knows that.

And he didn't run because of Charlottesville. He used that as an excuse to run.

TAPPER: President Biden?

BIDEN: And debunk. It happened. All you have to do is listen to what was said at the time.

And the idea that somehow that's the only reason I ran. I ran because I was worried a guy like this guy can get elected.

If he thought they were good people coming out of that all – that forest, carrying those – those woods, carrying those torches, then he didn't deserve to be president, didn't deserve to be president at all.

And the idea that he's talking about all of this being fabricated, we saw it with our own eyes. We saw what happened on January 6. We saw the people breaking through the windows. We saw people occupying there.

His own vice president – look, there's a reason why forty of his forty-four top cabinet officers refused to endorse him this time. His vice president hasn't endorsed him this time.

So, why? Why? They know him well. They serve with them. Why are they not endorsing him?

TAPPER: Thank you, President Biden. We're going to be right back with more from the CNN presidential debate.

The Real Debate Studio

STOSSEL: Again, there's no parallel question for you in there. But let me ask of these two gentlemen who would be worse as President?

KENNEDY: I mean, I think you, you put your nail, that you put that hammer on that nail perfectly. 70% of the American

47

public say they don't want this contest, because neither of them, neither of them are running on the things that are absolutely critical to Americans right now.

The only thing they have, the only argument they have is being scared of that other guy. He's a felon. He's a bad guy. He's going to destroy the Republic. They are running on fear. If Americans want to vote out of fear they're going to vote for these guys. If they want to vote out of hope they're going to vote on me.

Because I want to talk, I want to talk about the fact that 71% of the people in this country are making less than the cost of basic human needs.

I want to talk about the fact that under their administrations, the top 1% of Americans now own more than the, than the 60% represent the American middle class.

We, our country, has utterly changed because of them. I run into elderly people who are cutting their prescription pills in two to make it through the week. Mothers who are downgrading their purchases at the grocery store to make it out of the checkout line. A couple in, in New Hampshire who told me they are in their bedroom or in their living room with a crying baby, arguing each other about whether that baby is $50.00 sick or $100.00 sick or $500.00 sick before they bring it a hospital. These are kids who come up to me every day and say that one day a week, I have to choose between buying gasoline and buying lunch.

These are choices you're not supposed to have to make in this country and it's them, these two are not telling the American people how they're going to get our kids into homes and that's what I want to talk about.

STOSSEL: Back to CNN.

CNN STUDIO

BASH: Welcome back to the CNN Presidential Debate live from Georgia.

Let's talk about persistent challenges you both faced in your first terms, and you'd certainly face again in a second term.

President Biden, while Black unemployment dropped to a record low under your presidency, Black families still earn far less than White families.

Black mothers are still three times more likely to die from pregnancy related causes. And Black Americans are imprisoned at five times the rate of White Americans. What do you say to Black voters who are disappointed that you haven't made more progress?

BIDEN: They acknowledge we made a lot of progress, number one. The facts of the matter is more small Black businesses that have been started in any time in history. Number two, the wages of Black – Black unemployment is the lowest level it has been in a long, long time. Number three, we find them – they're trying to provide housing for Black Americans and dealing with segregation that exists among these corporate – these corporate operations that collude to keep people out of their houses.

And in addition to that, we find that the impact of, on the – the choice that Black families have to make relative to childcare is incredibly difficult. When we did the first major piece of legislation in the past, I was able to reduce Black childcare costs. I cut them in half, in half. We've got to make sure we provide for childcare costs. We've got to make sure – because when you provide that childcare protections, you increase economic growth because more people can be in the – in the job market.

So there's more to be done, considerably more to be done, but we've done a great deal so far and I'm not letting up and they know it.

BASH: You have forty-nine seconds left. What do you say to Black voters who are disappointed with the progress so far?

BIDEN: I say, I don't blame them for being disappointed. Inflation is still hurting them badly. For example, I provided for the idea that any Black family, first time home buyer should get a $10,000.00 tax credit to be able to buy their first home so they can get started.

I made sure that we're in a situation where all those Black families and those Black individuals who provided had to take out student loans that were ballooning, that if they were engaged in nursing and anything having to do with volunteerism, if they paid their bills for ten years on their student debt, all the rest was forgiven after ten years. Millions have benefited from that and we're going to do a whole lot more for Black families.

BASH: Thank you. President Trump?

TRUMP: And he caused the inflation. He's blaming inflation. And he's right, it's been very bad. He caused the inflation and it's killing Black families and Hispanic families and just about everybody. It's killing people. They can't buy groceries anymore. They can't.

You look at the cost of food where it's doubled and tripled and quadrupled. They can't live. They're not living anymore. He caused this inflation.

I gave him a country with no, essentially no inflation. It was perfect. It was so good. All he had to do is leave it alone. He destroyed it with his green new scam and all of the other – all this money that's being thrown out the window.

He caused inflation. As sure as you're sitting there, the fact is that his big kill on the Black people is the millions of people that he's allowed to come in through the border. They're taking Black jobs now and it could be eighteen. It could be nineteen and even 20 million people. They're taking Black jobs and they're taking Hispanic jobs and you haven't seen it yet, but you're going to see something that's going to be the worst in our history.

BASH: Thank you. President Biden?

BIDEN: There was no inflation when I became president. You know why? The economy was flat on its back. 15% unemployment. He decimated the economy, absolutely decimated the economy. That's why there was no inflation at the time.

There were no jobs. We provided thousands of millions of jobs for individuals who were involved in communities, including minority communities. We made sure that they have health insurance. We have covered with – the ACA has increased. I made sure that they're $8,000.00 per person in the family to get written off in health care, but this guy wants to eliminate that. They tried fifty times. He wants to get rid of the ACA again, and they're going to try again if they win.

You find ourselves in a position where the idea that we're not doing it. I put more – we put more police on the street than any administration has. He wants to cut the cops. We're providing for equity, equity, and making sure people have a shot to make it. There is a lot going on. But, on inflation, he caused it by his tremendous malfeasance in the way he handled the pandemic.

The Real Debate Studio

STOSSEL: So, trying to pass on a similar question. Um, I don't know why they single out Black people, but it's certainly true that some minorities in America do not do as well as us White people and should, should government do something about that.

KENNEDY: And I, you know, I agree with the assessment that inflation is disproportionately hurting Black people because there are wage earners. They've got disproportionately fixed income. The border is disproportionately hurting Black and Hispanic workers.

I hear that every single day I spent ten years working with Cesar Chavez during the last part of his life, he had two issues. One was pesticides, disproportionate impact of pesticides on Hispanics. The other issue was the border because he understood all of these illegal Americans coming across the border were hurting the capacity of his workers. American workers, you get good jobs and wages.

The issue that they didn't talk about two issues. One is education. We spend $50 billion a year on the Department of Education and Black kids in this country, it's a crime. What is happening to their schools when I was a kid, we had the best educated kids by every measure of any country in the world.

We're now twenty-two - we're throwing billions of dollars and in inner city schools, most of these kids cannot read or do math at great level. It is a crime. We need to give them choice. We need to give them charter schools, neither of them have done anything about it.

The last issue which both of them have aggravated is a mass incarceration crisis. One out of every four Black men has had some contact with the correctional service and 60% of the Blacks in American jails are there for nonviolent drug offenses. Why? Because President Biden Anti-Drug Abuse Act in 1986 that he wrote that gave one hundred times the penalty for crack cocaine as powder cocaine. It was designed to put Blacks in jail. Then he passed in 1994 omnibus crime bill with the super predatory provisions. The mandatory sentencing the three strikes you're out, those two bills double the amounts of Blacks in American prison. The amounts of Black in American prison were studies for the civil war

STOSSEL: Time is up. Back to CNN.

CNN STUDIO

BASH: Thank you. Another persistent challenge is the climate crisis. 2023 was the hottest year in recorded history, and communities across the country are confronting the devastating effects of extreme heat, intensifying wildfires, stronger hurricanes, and rising sea levels. Former President Trump, you've vowed to end your opponent's climate initiatives. But, will you take any action as president to slow the climate crisis?

TRUMP: Well, let me just go back to what he said about the police, how close the police are to him. Almost every police group in the nation from every state is supporting Donald J. Trump, almost every police group. And what he has done to the Black population is horrible, including the fact that for ten years he called them super predators. We can't, in the 1990s, we can't forget that. Super predators was his name, and he called it to them for ten years, and they've taken great offense at it, and now they see it happening.

But, when they see what I did for criminal justice reform and for the historically Black colleges and universities, where I funded them and got them all funded, and the opportunity zones with Tim. As you know, Tim Scott was - incredible, he did a great job, a great Senator from South Carolina. He came to me with the idea and it was a great idea. It's one of the most successful economic development acts ever in the country, opportunity zones. And the biggest beneficiary are Blacks. And that's why we have the best numbers with them in maybe ever, they're saying ever, I read this morning, wherever, the best numbers, he has lost much of the Black population because he has done a horrible job for Black people. He has also done a horrible job for Hispanics.

But, why do you see these millions of people pouring into our country and they're going to take the jobs? And it's already started. And you haven't seen anything yet. It's a disaster.

BASH: You've thirty-eight seconds left, President Trump. Will you take any action as President to slow the climate crisis?

TRUMP: So, I want absolutely immaculate clean water and I want absolutely clean air, and we had it. We had H_2O. We had the best numbers ever. And we did – we were using all forms of energy, all forms, everything. And yet, during my four years, I had the best environmental numbers ever. And my top environmental people gave me that statistic just before I walked on the stage, actually.

BIDEN: I don't know where the hell he has been. The idea that anything he said is true. I've passed the most extensive, it was the most extensive climate change legislation in history, in history. We find ourselves – and by the way, Black colleges, I came up with $50 billion for HBCUs, historic Black universities and colleges, because they don't have the kind of contributors that they have to build these laboratories and the like. Any Black student is capable in college in doing what any White student can do. They just have the money. But now, they'll be able to get those jobs in high tech.

We're in a situation where the idea that he is claiming to have done something that had the cleanest water, the cleanest water? He had not done a damn thing with the environment. He – out of the Paris Peace Accord – Climate Accord, I immediately joined it, because if we reach for 1.5 degrees Celsius at any one point, well, there is no way back. The only existential threat to humanity is climate change. And he didn't do a damn thing about it. He wants to undo all that I've done.

TRUMP: The Paris Accord was going to cost us a trillion dollars, and China nothing, and Russia nothing, and India nothing. It was a rip-off of the United States. And I ended it because I didn't want to waste that money because they treat us horribly. We were the only ones – it was costing us money. Nobody else was paying into it. And it was a disaster.

But, everything that he said just now, I'll give you an example. I heard him say before insulin, I'm the one that got the insulin down for the seniors. I took care of the seniors. What he is doing is destroying all of our medical programs because the migrants coming in. They want everybody. And look, I have the biggest heart on the stage. I guarantee you that. And I want to take care of people. But, we're destroying our country. They're taking over our schools, our hospitals, and they're going to be taking over Social Security. He is destroying Social Security, Medicare and Medicaid.

BIDEN: The idea is that we, in fact – we were the only ones of consequence or not who are not members of the Paris Accord. How can we do anything when we're not able to – the United States can't get it's pollution under control? One of the largest polluters in the world, number one. We're making significant progress. By 2035, we will have cut pollution in half. We have – we have made significant progress. And we're continuing to make progress.

We set up a Climate Corps for thousands of young people will learn how to deal with climate, just like the Peace Corps. And we're going to – we're moving in directions that are going to significantly change the elements of the cause of pollution.

But the idea, that he claims that, he has the biggest heart up here and he's really concerned about – about pollution and about climate, I've not seen any indication of that.

And, by the way, with regard to prescription drugs, one company agreed that they would reduce the price to $35.00, which I was calling for – one, voluntarily. I made sure every company in the world, every pharmaceutical company, cannot have to pay.

BASH: Thank you.

BIDEN: And, by the way...

The Real Debate Studio

STOSSEL: Oh, this is frustrating. Um this is your specialty, but I object to CNN's biased question. Would you take any action to slow the climate crisis that assumes climate change is a crisis? So, do you think it is? And what would you do?

KENNEDY: I think climate change first, first I want to say this. There's been nobody who's ever run for President United States and gotten anywhere, well, let's say I'll even say it more definitely who has a strong environmental record and a, a larger commitment to the environment. And I do, it's what I've been doing for forty years. I believe climate change is existential. Um, but I don't insist other people believe that. And I think we, I focus and I've always focused on market based solutions which I think are the most efficient, eliminating subsidies for the energy industry. For the particularly carbon. We give carbon $5.2 trillion in subsidies a year and creating a national grid system that is robust enough to do long haul transportation of electrons that then and we turn every American into an energy entrepreneur, every home into a power plant, with the cheapest, most efficient forms of energy.

The market we need to start by protecting habitat, our air, water, wetlands, soils. That's the most important thing you can do for climate. It's almost altogether ignored. President Biden's program which is the Inflation Reduction Act does a few good things, but the bulk of it is large subsidies to the oil industry and to Blackrock and other really sinister corporations or carbon capture, which is boondoggle. Carbon capture is a boondoggle. We should not be funding it, we should not be encouraging it. We shouldn't be encouraging any kind of geoengineering of that kind.

We should be, we should be focusing on restoring our soils, doing regenerative agriculture, protecting our air, our water, our wildlife, stopping the carbon, stopping the carbon discharge from coal burning power plants which are causing a half a trillion dollars in respiratory injuries annually, poisoning every freshwater fish in our country with mercury.

STOSSEL: Sorry, your time is up, back to CNN.

CNN STUDIO

TAPPER: So every day, millions of Americans struggle just to make ends meet. For many older Americans, Social Security provides a critical lifeline.

President Biden, if nothing is done to Social Security, seniors will see their benefits cut in just over ten years. Will you name tonight one specific step that you're willing to take to keep Social Security solvent?

BIDEN: Yes, make the very wealthy begin to pay their fair share. Right now, everybody making under $170,000.00 pays 6% of their income, of their paycheck, every single time they get a paycheck, from the time of the first one they get when they're eighteen years old.

The idea that they're going to – I'm not – I've been proposing that everybody, they pay – millionaires pay 1% – 1%. So no one after – I would not raise the cost of Social Security for anybody under $400,000.00. After that, I begin to make the wealthy begin to pay their fair share, by increasing from 1% beyond, to be able to guarantee the program for life.

TAPPER: So you still have eighty-two seconds left. Are there any other measures that you think that would be able to help keep Social Security solvent, or is just – is that one enough?

BIDEN: Well, that one enough will keep it solvent. But the biggest thing I'll do, if we defeat this man, because he wants to get rid of Social Security; he thinks that there's plenty to cut in Social Security. He's wanting to cut Social Security and Medicare, both times. And that's with – and if you look at the program put forward by the House Republican Caucus that he, I believe, supports, is in fact wanting to cut it as well.

The idea that we don't need to protect our seniors is ridiculous. We put – and, by the way, the American public has greater health care coverage today than ever before. And under the ACA, as I said, you're in a circumstance where 400,000 people – I mean, 40 million people – would not have insurance because they have a pre-existing condition. The only thing that allows them to have that insurance is the fact that they in fact are part of the ACA.

And, by the way, the other thing is we're in a situation where I talk about education for Black communities. I've raised the number, the amount of money for Pell grants by another $8,000.00 for anybody making under $70,000.00 a year, are going to be able to get $15,000.00 towards their tuition.

It's just – he – he just doesn't know what he's talking about.

TAPPER: Thank you, President Biden. President Trump?

TRUMP: So I've dealt with politicians all my life. I've been on this side of the equation for the last eight years. I've never seen anybody lie like this guy. He lies – I've never seen it. He could look you in the face. So – and about so many other things, too.

And we mentioned the laptop, we mentioned "Russia, Russia, Russia", "Ukraine, Ukraine, Ukraine." And everything he does is a lie. It's misinformation and disinformation. The "losers and suckers" story that he made up is a total lie on the military. It's a disgrace.

But Social Security, he's destroying it. Because millions of people are pouring into our country, and they're putting them on to Social Security; they're putting them on to Medicare, Medicaid. They're putting them in our hospitals. They're taking the place of our citizens.

They're – what they're doing to the V.A., to our veterans, is unbelievable. Our veterans are living in the street and these people are living in luxury hotels. He doesn't know what he's doing. And it – it's really coming back. I've never seen such anger in our country before.

TAPPER: President Biden?

BIDEN: The idea that veterans are not being taken care of, I told you before – and, by the way, when I said, "suckers and losers," he said – he acknowledged after it that he fired that general. That general got fired because he's the one that acknowledged that that's what he said. He was the one standing with Trump when he said it, number one.

Number two, the idea that we're going to be in a situation where all these millions and millions, the way he talks about it, illegal aliens are coming into the country and taking away our jobs, there's a reason why we have the fastest-growing economy in the world, a reason why we have the most successful economy in the world. We're doing better than any other nation in the world.

And, by the way, those fifteen Nobel laureates he talked about being phony, those fifteen Nobel laureates, economists, they all said that, if Trump is re-elected, we're likely to have a recession, and inflation is going to increasingly go up.

And by the way, worst president in history – one hundred and fifty-nine presidential scholars voted him the worst president in the history of the United States of America.

The Real Debate Studio

STOSSEL: Again, a very important question Dodged. Social security is going bankrupt, taxing the rich more won't solve it. What would you cut or what would you do?

KENNEDY: Well, you know, and I agree with you and Social Security is not entitlement. Social Security is a contract, workers put 6% of their income into a, you know, into a fund. And they're told that at sixty-five, they're going to get that money back. It's not a, it's not a, it's not an entitlement. It is contractual and the government, the United States would be outrageous if the United States did not live up to its full faith and credit of paying back those obligations even if it has to reach outside of the Social Security system to get it.

And what we need to be doing is winding down our military commitment. We need to unravel the war machine. We need to solve our chronic disease epidemic, which is the biggest cause 4.3 trillion and we can do those things very quickly. I'm going to cut the military budget in half during my first four years. I'm going to use AI and blockchain to eliminate waste in government to save more money. And I'm going to get rid of the chronic disease epidemic.

And ultimately that's going to save us a lot of money. And this has to be a priority for us. I, I, I also want to say this. I was astonished by President Biden's claim that we have the best economy in the world. We have, you know I see kids everyday. None of this generation is going to get into a home and that's going to destroy the American middle class. The American middle class is the greatest economic engine in the history of mankind.

When I was a kid, our country owned half the wealth in the face of the earth. And it was largely because one, we had industrial base after World War II. But most importantly, we got every American into a home, and because they were in a home, they had equity, they could borrow money, they could bet it on a business and that's what's going to drive our economy.

STOSSEL: Back to CNN.

CNN STUDIO

TAPPER: President Biden, thank you so much. Let's turn to the cost of childcare, which many American families struggle to afford.

President Trump, both you and President Biden have tried to address this issue, but the average cost of childcare in this country has risen to more than $11,000.00 a year per child. For many families, the cost of childcare for two children is more than their rent. In your second term, what would you do to make childcare more affordable?

TRUMP: Just to go back. The general got fired because he was no good. And if he said that, that's why he made it up. But we have nineteen people that said I didn't say it, and they're very highly respected, much more so than him.

The other thing is, he doesn't fire people. He never fired people. I've never seen him fire anybody. I did fire a lot. I fired Comey because he was no good. I fired a lot of the top people at the FBI, drained the swamp. They were no good. Not easy to fire people. You'd pay a price for it, but they were no good. I inherited these people. I didn't put him there. I didn't put Comey there. He was no good. I fired him.

This guy hasn't fired anybody. He never fires. He should have fired every military man that was involved with that Afghan – the Afghanistan horror show. The most embarrassing moment in the history of our country. He didn't fire? Did you fire anybody? Did you fire anybody that's on the border, that's allowed us to have the worst border in the history of the world? Did anybody get fired for allowing 18 million people, many from prisons, many from mental institutions? Did you fire anybody that allowed our country to be destroyed? Joe, our country is being destroyed as you and I sit up here and waste a lot of time on this debate. This shouldn't be a debate.

He is the worst president. He just said it about me because I said it. But look, he's the worst president in the history of our country. He's destroyed our country. Now, all of a sudden, he's trying to get a little tough on the border. He come out – came out with a nothing deal, and it reduced it a little bit. A little bit, like this much. It's insignificant.

He wants open borders. He wants our country to either be destroyed or he wants to pick up those people as voters. And I don't think – we just can't let it happen. If he wins this election, our country doesn't have a chance. Not even a chance of coming out of this rut. We probably won't have a country left anymore. That's how bad it is. He is the worst in history by far.

TAPPER: Thank you, President Trump. President Biden?

BIDEN: We are the most admired country in the world. We're the United States of America. There's nothing beyond our capacity. We have the finest military in the history of the world. The finest in the history of the world. No one thinks we're weak. No one wants to screw around with us. Nobody. Number one.

Number two, the idea that we're talking about worst presidents. I wasn't joking. Look it up. Go online. One hundred and fifty-nine or fifty-eight, don't hold me to the exact number, presidential historians. They've had meetings and they voted who's the worst president in American history. One through best to worst. They said he was the worst in all of American history. That's a fact. That's not conjecture. He can argue they are wrong, but that's what they voted.

The idea that he is knowing – doing anything to deal with childcare. He did very – virtually nothing to childcare. We should significantly increase the childcare tax credit. We should significantly increase the availability of women and men for child or single parents to be able to go back to work, and we should encourage businesses to hold – to have childcare facilities.

TAPPER: Thank you, President Biden. President Trump, the question was about what would you do to make childcare more affordable? If you want to take your minute.

TRUMP: Just you understand, we have polling. We have other things that do – they rate him the worst because what he's done is so bad. And they rate me – yes, I'll show you. I will show you. And they rate me one of the best. Okay.

And if I'm given another four years, I will be the best. I think I'll be the best. Nobody's ever created an economy like us. Nobody ever cut taxes like us. He's the only one I know. He wants to raise your taxes by four times. He wants to raise everybody's taxes by four times. He wants the Trump tax cuts to expire so everybody, including the two of you are going to pay four to five times. Nobody ever heard of this before.

All my life I'd grow up and I'd see politicians talking about cutting taxes. When we cut taxes, as I said, we did more business. Apple and all these companies, they were bringing money back into our country. The worst president in history by far, and everybody knows it.

TAPPER: President Biden?

BIDEN: Look, the fact of the matter is that he's dead wrong about it. He's increased the tariff – he's increased – he will increase the taxes on middle class people. I said I'd never raise a tax on anybody making less than $400,000.00. I didn't.

But this tariff, this 10% tariffs. Everything coming into the country, you know what the economists say? That's going to cost the average American $2,500.00 a year and more, because they're going to have to pay the difference in food and all the things that are very important.

Number two, he's in a situation where he talks about how he has not raised – he somehow helped the middle class. The middle class has been devastated by you. Now you want a new tax cut of $5 trillion over the next ten years, which is going to fundamentally bankrupt the country. You had the largest deficit of any president in American history, number one.

Number two, you have not, in fact, made any contact, any progress with China. We are the lowest trade deficit with China since 2010.

TAPPER: Thank you, President Biden. Thank you, President Biden.

The Real Debate Studio

STOSSEL: Back to their original question, um, CNN has somehow found a childcare crisis in America. Somehow Americans raised children for years. Now, there's a crisis because it costs too much. That's something government did or can fix?

KENNEDY: Well, the reason there is a crisis is because the economy with the middle class is gone. So in order to pay for a home, you need two jobs or three jobs. So oftentimes, I'm running into people of four jobs between the couple. A couple used to be when you and I were growing up, mom stayed at home, or a parent stayed at home and took care of the kids. That doesn't happen anymore. Now, both parents in order to hold on to that home need to be working. So we do have a child-care crisis in this country and it's because of the destruction that both these men contributed to of the American middle class and neither of them is offering any way to restore the middle class.

Childcare for the Black Americans, John, is 37% of income, a single child. Oh, and nobody can afford that. And what I'm gonna do, I'm gonna wind out, I'm going to balance our budget which is what President Trump promised to do, but I'm actually going to do it because why? Because it's existential if we don't have the courage to do that, no matter what the cuts are, we have to do that or we are going to cease to exist as an influential nation.

I'm going to, but you cannot, we cannot cut our way out of this debt. We have to, we have to build new industry, we have to build GDP. And one of the most efficient ways of building GDP is through childcare. We guarantee childcare. There's a 22%, twenty-two times return on investment. As I said, every million dollar we spend on military weapons creates two jobs. Every million dollars we spend on childcare creates tenty-two jobs and we need to grow our way out of this budget death spiral. And one of the ways we're going to do that is by providing childcare by, by taking away half a trillion dollars from the military.

STOSSEL: Back to the CNN.

CNN STUDIO

Let's discuss an epidemic impacting millions of Americans that both of you have made a top priority in your first term, the opioid crisis. And for both of you, the number of overdose deaths in this country has gone up. Under your term, it went up. Under your term, it has gone up.

Former President Trump, despite the efforts that both of you have made, more than 100,000 Americans are dying from overdoses every year, primarily from fentanyl and other opioids. What will you do to help Americans right now in the throes of addiction, who are struggling to get the treatment they need?

TRUMP: To finish up, we now have the largest deficit in the history of our country under this guy, we have the largest deficit with China. He gets paid by China. He's a Manchurian candidate. He gets money from China. So I think he's afraid to deal with them or something.

But do you notice? He never took out my tariffs because we bring in so much money with the tariffs that I imposed on China. He never took them away. He can't because it's too much money. It's tremendous. And we saved our steel industries. And there was more to come, but he hasn't done that.

But he hasn't cut the tariffs because he can't, because it's too much money. But he's got the largest deficit in the history of our country, and he's got the worst situation with China. China is going to own us if you keep allowing them to do what they're doing to us as a country. They are killing us as a country, Joe, and you can't let that happen. You're destroying our country.

TAPPER: So, President Trump, you have sixty-seven seconds left. The question was, what are you going to do to help Americans in the throes of addiction right now who are struggling to get the treatment they need?

TRUMP: Jake, we were doing very well at addiction until the COVID came along. We had the two-and-a-half, almost three years of like nobody's ever had before, any country in every way. And then we had to get tough. And it was – the drugs pouring across the border, we're – it started to increase.

We got great equipment. We bought the certain dog. That's the most incredible thing that you've ever seen, the way they can spot it. We did a lot. And we had – we were getting very low numbers. Very, very low numbers.

Then he came along. The numbers – have you seen the numbers now? It's not only the 18 million people that I believe is even low, because the gotaways, they don't even talk about gotaways. But the numbers of – the amount of drugs and human trafficking in women coming across our border, the worst thing I've ever seen, at numbers nobody's ever seen under him because the border is so bad. But the number of drugs coming across our border now is the largest we've ever had by far.

TAPPER: President Trump, thank you. President Biden?

BIDEN: Fentanyl and the byproducts of fentanyl went down, for a while. And I wanted to make sure we use the machinery that can detect fentanyl, these big machines that roll over everything that comes across the border, and it costs a lot of money. That was part of this deal we put together, this bipartisan deal.

More fentanyl machines were able to detect drugs, more numbers of agents, more numbers of all the people at the border. And when we had that deal done, he went – he called his Republican colleagues said don't do it. It's going to hurt me politically.

He never argued it's not a good bill. It's a really good bill. We need those machines. We need those machines. And we're coming down very hard in every country in Asia in terms of precursors for fentanyl. And Mexico is working with us to make sure they don't have the technology to be able to put it together. That's what we have to do. We need those machines.

TAPPER: Thank you, President Biden. President Trump, and again, the question is about Americans in the throes of addiction right now struggling to get the treatment they need.

TRUMP: Because this does pertain to it. He ended remain in Mexico, he ended catch and release. I made it catch and release in Mexico, not catch and release here. We had so many things that we had done, hard negotiations with Mexico, and I got it all for nothing.

It's just like when you have a hostage, we always pay $6 billion for a – every time he sees hostage. Now we have a hostage. A Wall Street Journal reporter, I think a good guy, and he's over there because Putin is laughing at this guy, probably asking for billions of dollars for the reporter.

I will have him out very quickly, as soon as I take office, before I take office. I said by literally, as soon as I win the election, I will have that reporter out. He should have had him out a long time ago. But Putin is probably asking for billions and billions of dollars because this guy pays it every time.

We had two cases where we paid $6 billion for five people. I got fifty-eight people out, and I paid essentially nothing.

TAPPER: Thank you, President Trump.

Dana.

The Real Debate Studio

STOSSEL: I like it when they cut them off on CNN. The question, we do have a big opioid problem. People in crisis, people overdosing, but also people in pain who can't get pain relief because doctors are afraid of the DEA, what would you do?

KENNEDY: Both of these Presidents missed the point. Um they're talking about drug interdiction at the border. That's not the problem, in fact, even if you sealed the border or virtually sealed it, fentanyl is, it occupies such a tiny volume, about one two hundredth of other opioids, you could bring enough fentanyl across the border in a briefcase to kill everybody in Los Angeles. So, the fentanyl is going to come in this country.

The problem is something much larger than that. It's the, it's the alien, it's a generation that is alienated, that is dispossessed, that is depressed, it is suicidal, that is disconnected from community and that's why they're turning to drugs, and we need to deal with that problem and we need to reduce demand and that my, signature policy.

(applause)

STOSSEL: Thank you..

KENNEDY: It is to begin taxing marijuana federally by the scheduler, um schedule one where it is now where the federal government is not allowed to tax it. So marijuana is legal in many states, but the federal government cannot collect taxes on it. It's legal, it's not whether you can tax it or not. It's not going to affect the number of people who are using it or amount that's used. We're going to de schedule it so the government can start collecting taxes that will raise $8.5 billion in revenue. I'm going to dedicate that money. The building drug rehabilitation farms, wellness farms, restoration farms in rural areas all over this country where any American go for free to deal with depression, suicidal behavior, alcoholism, drug addiction, to illegal drugs, but also addiction to SSRI's the Benzos, Adderall. We need to reclaim our children. If a whole generation that is growing up with social media, it's growing up with no hope for their future, it can't get into homes, they can't get meeting...

STOSSEL: That stops two minutes, Mr. Kennedy. Back to CNN.

CNN STUDIO

BASH: Let's turn to concerns that voters have about each of you.

President Biden, you would be eighty-six at the end of your second term. How do you address concerns about your capability to handle the toughest job in the world well into your 80s?

BIDEN: Well, first of all, I spent half my career being – being criticized being the youngest person in politics. I was the second-youngest person ever elected to the United States Senate. And now I'm the oldest. This guy's three years younger and a lot less competent. I think that just look at the record. Look what I've done. Look how I've turned around the horrible situation he left me.

As I said, 50 million new jobs, 800,000 manufacturing jobs, more investment in America, over millions – billions of dollars in private investment and – and enterprises that we are growing. We've – by the way, we brought an awful a lot of people – the whole idea of computer chips. We used to have 40% of the market. We invented those chips. And we lost it because he was sending people to cheap – to find the cheapest jobs overseas and to bring home a product.

So I went – I went to South Korea. I convinced Samsung to invest billions of dollars here in the United States. And then guess what? Those fabs, they call them, to – to build these chips, those fabs pay over $100,000.00. You don't need a college degree for them. And there's billions, about $40 billion dollars already being invested and being built right now in the United States, creating significant jobs for Americans all over – from all over the world.

BASH: President Biden, you have forty seconds left. Would you like to add anything?

BIDEN: Yeah, I would. The idea that somehow we are this failing country, I never heard a president talk like this before. We – we're the envy of the world. Name me a single major country president who wouldn't trade places with the United States of America. For all our problems and all our opportunities, we're the most progressive country in the world in getting things done. We're the strongest country in the world. We're a country in the world who keeps our word and everybody trusts us, all of our allies.

And our – those who he cuddles up to, from Kim Jong-Un who he sends love letters to, or Putin, et cetera, they don't want to screw around with us.

BASH: Thank you.

Former President Trump, to follow up, you would be eighty-two at the end of your second term. What do you say to voters who have concerns about your capabilities to serve?

TRUMP: Well, I took two tests, cognitive tests. I aced them, both of them, as you know. We made it public. He took none. I'd like to see him take one, just one, a real easy one. Like go through the first five questions, he couldn't do it. But I took two cognitive tests. I took physical exams every year. And, you know, we knock on wood, wherever we may have wood, that I'm in very good health. I just won two club championships, not even senior, two regular club championships. To do that, you have to be quite smart and you have to be able to hit the ball a long way. And I do it. He doesn't do it. He can't hit a ball fifty yards. He challenged me to a golf match. He can't hit a ball fifty yards.

I think I'm a very good shape. I feel that I'm in as good a shape as I was twenty-five, thirty years ago. Actually, I'm probably a little bit lighter. But I'm in as good a shape as I was years ago. I feel very good. I feel the same.

But I took – I was willing to take a cognitive test. And you know what, if I didn't do well – I aced them. Dr. Ronny Jackson, who's a great guy, when he was White House doctor. And then I took another one, a similar one, and both – one of them said they'd never seen anybody ace them.

BASH: Thank you. President Biden?

BIDEN: You're going to see he's six-foot-five and only two hundred and twenty-five pounds – or two hundred and thirty-five pounds.

TRUMP: (inaudible).

BIDEN: Well, you said six-four, two hundred...

TRUMP: (inaudible).

BIDEN: Well, anyway, that's – anyway, just take a look at what he says he is and take a look at what he is.

Look, I'd be happy to have a driving contest with him. I got my handicap, which, when I was vice president, down to a six.

And by the way, I told you before I'm happy to play golf if you carry your own bag. Think you can do it?

TRUMP: That's the biggest lie, that he's a six handicap, of all.

BIDEN: I was eight handicap.

TRUMP: Yeah.

BIDEN: Eight, but I have – you know how many...

TRUMP: I've seen your swing, I know your swing.

(CROSSTALK)

BASH: President Trump, we're going to...

(CROSSTALK)

TRUMP: Let's not act like children.

BIDEN: You are a child.

The Real Debate Studio

STOSSEL: Merciful when they cut them off.

KENNEDY: Now all I got to say is, I hope they let me on the stage for that contest.

(Crowd laughing and applauding)

STOSSEL: What do you do to stay healthy?

KENNEDY: What?

STOSSEL: What do you do to stay healthy?

KENNEDY: What do I?

STOSSEL: What do you do to stay healthy?

KENNEDY: What do I do? I, well, I, uh I hike every day. I go to the gym every day. I, I don't ever eat processed food and I do intermittent fasting, and I try to eat well. So, I feel like I really want to be part of that contest.

STOSSEL: Back to CNN

(audience laughing)

CNN STUDIO

BASH: To you (Trump), a specific concern that voters have about you. Will you pledge tonight that once all legal challenges have been exhausted that you will accept the results of this election regardless of who wins and you will say right now that political violence in any form is unacceptable?

TRUMP: Well, I shouldn't have to say that, but, of course, I believe that. It's totally unacceptable. And if you would see my statements that I made on Twitter at the time, and also my statement that I made in the Rose Garden, you would say it's one of the strongest statements you've ever seen.

In addition to the speech I made, in front of, I believe, the largest crowd I've ever spoken to, and I will tell you, nobody ever talks about that. They talk about a relatively small number of people that went to the Capitol. And in many cases were ushered in by the police.

And as Nancy Pelosi said, it was her responsibility, not mine. She said that loud and clear.

But the answer is, if the election is fair free, and I want that more than anybody.

And I'll tell you something – I wish he was a great president because I wouldn't be here right now. I'd be at one of my many places enjoying myself. I wouldn't be under indictment because I wouldn't have been his political oppon... – you know, opponent. Because he indicted me because I was his opponent.

I wish he was a great president. I would rather have that.

I wouldn't be here. I don't mind being here, but the only reason I'm here is he's so bad as a president, that I'm going to make America great again. We're going to make America great again.

We're a failing nation right now. We're a seriously failing nation. And we're a failing nation because of him.

His policies are so bad. His military policies are insane. They're insane.

These are wars that will never end with him. He will drive us into World War III and we're closer to World War III than anybody can imagine. We are very, very close to World War III, and he's driving us there.

And Kim Jong-Un, and President Xi of China – Kim Jong-Un of North Korea, all of these – Putin – they don't respect him. They don't fear him. They have nothing going with this gentleman and he's going to drive us into World War III.

BIDEN: If you want a World War III, let him follow and win, and let Putin say, do what you want to NATO – just do what you want.

There's a thing called Article Five, an attack on one is attack on all, a required response.

The idea – the idea – I can't think of a single major leader in the world who wouldn't trade places with what job I've done and what they've done, because we are a powerful nation, we have wonderful peace, because of the people, not me, because of the American people. They're capable of anything and they step up when they're needed.

And right now, we're needed. We're needed to protect the world because our own safety is at stake.

And again, you want to have war, just let Putin go ahead and take Kyiv, make sure they move on, see what happens in Poland, Hungary, and other places along that border. Then you have a war.

BASH: President Trump, as I come back to you for a follow-up. The question was, will you accept the results of this election regardless of who wins?

TRUMP: Just to finish what he said, if I might, Russia – they took a lot of land from Bush. They took a lot of land from Obama and Biden. They took no land, nothing, from Trump, nothing.

He knew not to do it. He's not going to play games with me. He knew that. I got along with him very well, but he knew not to play games.

He took nothing from me, but now, he's going to take the whole thing from this man right here.

That's a war that should have never started. It would've never started ever with me. And he's going to take Ukraine and, you know, you asked me a question before, would you do this with – he's got us in such a bad position right now with Ukraine and Russia because Ukraine's not winning that war.

He said, I will never settle until such time – they're running out of people, they're running out of soldiers, they've lost so many people. It's so sad.

They've lost so many people and they've lost those gorgeous cities with the golden domes that are a thousand years old, all because of him and stupid decisions.

Russia would've never attacked if I were president.

BASH: President Trump, the question was, will you accept the results of the election regardless of who wins? Yes or no, please?

TRUMP: If it's a fair and legal and good election – absolutely. I would have much rather accepted these, but the fraud and everything else was ridiculous that if you want, we'll have a news conference on it in a week or we'll have another one of these on – in a week.

But I will absolutely – there's nothing I'd rather do. It would be much easier for me to do that than I'm running again. I wasn't really going to run until I saw the horrible job he did. He's destroying our country.

I would be very happy to be someplace else, in a nice location someplace. And again, no indictments, no political opponent's stuff, because it's the only way he thinks he can win.

But unfortunately, it's driven up by numbers and driven it up to a very high level, because the people understand it.

BIDEN: Let's see what your numbers are when this election is over.

TRUMP: We'll see.

BIDEN: Let's see. You're a whiner. When you lost the first time, you continued to appeal and appeal to courts all across the country.

Not one single court in America said any of your claims had any merit, state or local, none.

But you continue to promote this lie about somehow there's all this misrepresentation, all the stealing. There's no evidence of that at all.

And I tell you what, I doubt whether you'll accept it because you're such a whiner. The idea if you lose again, you're accepting anything, you can't stand the loss. Something snapped in you when you lost the last time.

The Real Debate Studio

STOSSEL: And that's it for the CNN Debate. You, this is your forum, you get the final word, but just one observation is that listening to them, American is in terrible decline, but I don't see people risking their lives to leave America or go to many other countries. They want to come here and you say the middle class is disappearing. It's true. It's getting smaller. But the data show mostly because they're going into the upper class. I think America is doing pretty well and we just need you politicians to leave us alone.

KENNEDY: I don't want to make an observation about President Trump's final point. Which I think is a very, very important point for Americans to understand. We are closer to nuclear war right now than at any time since 1962.

This week, we did something extraordinary that was hardly covered by the press which is we fired a missile in coordination with the Ukraine, into a series of missiles, into Crimea with cluster bombs which every nation in the world except for us and North Korea says is a war crime. We dropped them on as a civilian population, people who were sitting on sunning themselves on a beach and we killed a lot of children.

And, the previous week, Russians are in Cuba firing missiles because they've warned us we are going to win- lose of the war in Ukraine. Well, I've said that from the beginning. We cannot beat Russia in the Ukraine. They will, they cannot allow themselves to lose that war. They've been invaded three times through Ukraine.

The last time they were invaded, the Russians killed, or Hitler killed, one out of every seven Russians. They're not going to let us put NATO in Ukraine. They cannot do it. It's absolutely critical for their national security and we need to recognize that and we are pushing toward a war with a nuclear power that says they will use a nuclear weapon if they're pushed to the edge, they have 2,500 more nuclear weapons than we do. They have better defensive weapons and we cannot fight a world war anymore because of hypersonic missiles. We couldn't get a million men across the Atlantic, even worse. We do not have an industrial base like we did before World War II, we can't create weapons anymore. We create small numbers but nothing like the Chinese or the Russians.

This is, this is something that every American needs to understand how close the incompetence of this administration has brought us to war. I'll shut up.

STOSSEL: Closing statements...

KENNEDY: Now, I mean.

STOSSEL: We have closing statement from...

KENNEDY: Can I say...

STOSSEL: You'll get your closing statement right after they get theirs.

KENNEDY: Sorry.

CNN STUDIO

TAPPER: It is now time for the candidates to deliver their closing statements.

As predetermined by a coin toss, we're going to begin with you, President Biden. You have two minutes.

BIDEN: We've made significant progress from the debacle that was left by President Trump in his – in his last term.

We find ourselves in a situation where, number one, we have to make sure that we have a fair tax system. I ask anyone out there in the audience, or anyone out watching this debate, do you think the tax system is fair?

The fact is that I said, nobody even making under $400,000.00 had a single penny increase in their taxes and it will not. And if I'm reelected, that'll be the case again.

But this guy is – has increased your taxes because of the deficit. Number one, he's increased inflation because of the debacle he left after – when he handled the pandemic. And he finds himself in a position where he now wants to tax you more by putting a 10% tariff on everything that comes into the United States America.

What I did, when, for example, he wants to get away with – and get rid of the ability of Medicare to – for the ability to – for the – us to be able to negotiate drug prices with big pharma companies.

Well, guess what? We got it – we got it down to $15.00 – excuse me, $35.00 for insulin instead of $400.00. No more than $2,000.00 for every senior no matter what they – how much prescription they need.

You know what that did? That reduced the federal deficit – debt by $160 billion over ten years because the government doesn't have to pay the exorbitant prices.

I'm going to make that available to every senior, all – or go longer. It's happening now, and everybody in America. He wants to get rid of that.

We have – I'm going to make sure we have childcare. We're going to significantly increase the credit people have for child-care. I'm going to make sure we do something about what we're doing on lead pipes and all the things that are causing health problems for people across the country.

We're going to continue to fight to bring down inflation and give people a break.

TAPPER: Thank you, President Biden. President Trump, you now have two minutes for your closing statement.

TRUMP: Like so many politicians, this man is just a complainer. He said, 'we want to do this, we want to do that, we want to get rid of this tax, that tax', but he doesn't do anything. He doesn't do.

All he does is make our country unsafe by allowing millions and millions of people to pour in. Our military doesn't respect him. We look like fools in Afghanistan.

We didn't stop – Israel, it was such a horrible thing that would have never happened. It should have never happened.

Iran was broke. Anybody that did business with Iran, including China, they couldn't do business with the United States. They all passed.

Iran was broke. They had no money for Hamas or Hezbollah, for terror, no money whatsoever.

Again, Ukraine should have never happened.

He talks about all this stuff, but he didn't do it. For three-and-a-half years, we're living in hell. We have the Palestinians, and we have everybody else rioting all over the place.

You talk about Charlottesville. This is a hundred times Charlottesville, a thousand times.

The whole country is exploding because of you, because they don't respect you. And they have to respect their president and they don't respect you throughout the world.

What we did was incredible. We re – rebuilt the military. We got the largest tax cut in history, the largest regulation cut in history.

The reason he's got jobs is because I cut the regulations that gave jobs, but he's putting a lot of those regulations back on.

All of the things that we've done, nobody's ever – never seen anything like – even from a medical standpoint. Right to Try, where we can try Space Age materials instead of going to Asia or going to Europe and trying to get when you're terminally ill.

Now, you can go and you can get something. You sign a document. They've been trying to get it for forty-two years.

But you know what we did for the military was incredible. Choice for our soldiers, where our soldiers, instead of waiting for three months to see a doctor, can go out and get themselves fixed up and readied up, and take care of themselves and they're living. And that's why I had the highest approval rating of the history of the V.A.

So, all of these things – we're in a failing nation, but it's not going to be failing anymore. We're going to make it great again.

BASH: Thank you, former President Trump, President Biden.

The Real Debate Studio

STOSSEL: And he ran out of time. Mr. Kennedy, two minutes closing statement.

KENNEDY: In 2013, there was a poll taken that asked young people under thirty-five in this country. Are you proud of the United States and 85% said yes. Same poll taken five months ago, 18% said yes.

So somehow during the administration of these two presidents, an entire generation of Americans has lost pride in our country and a hope in their own futures. And they, they feel that way because they see what's happening. They can't get into a home.

First generation in history in America that is gonna live worse lives than their parents. They see the vitriol that you saw here, the division, the polarization that makes them disgusted with politics. They are seeing the corrupt merger of state and corporate power that has transformed our agencies from the CIA, the health agencies, the environmental agencies into sock puppets, the industries they are supposed to regulate.

They are seeing the destruction of our soils, the destruction of our air and water watching this happen and the politicians do nothing about it except for hate on each other. If you want more of the same, you should vote for President Biden, President Trump. You know what's gonna happen. You know that. You know what they're gonna give you four more years of the same stuff.

If you want things to completely change, you're gonna support me, because I'm gonna change everything. And this, this is a moral fight. This is a moral battle for the soul of our nation to restore our moral authority around the world by protecting economic power abroad rather than spending $8 trillion on regime change, wars that have left every nation we've touched worse off than we found it.

And restoring our moral authority here at home. The first day in office, I'm going, you heard what they're gonna do. You don't even understand it. Here's what I'm gonna do. Day one in office, I'm going to issue an executive order, saying any federal official who tells a lie to the American public will lose his job.

Oh, I'm gonna stop, I'm gonna stop the surveillance state. I'm going to stop the propagandizing by our agencies of the American public. I'm going to unravel the war machine. I'm going to unravel the corrupt merger of state and corporate power. I know how to do it. I've been litigating against these agencies for years and I'm uniquely suited to do this, but I can tell you, I'm going to do these things when I get in there.

I'm gonna make sure that our constitution is protected that AI is deployed to make government more transparent rather than by government to enslave the rest of us. I'm gonna bring AI home and Blockchain home because we need these new industries to grow our way out of the debt crisis. This is something that these two aren't even talking about.

But if you want everything to change, you will support me. If you want to vote out of fear, you need to support one of those guys. If you wanna vote out of hope, out of inspiration, out of pride in your country, out of restoring the moral backbone of our people and our nation, you should vote for me. Thank you.

STOSSEL: The crowd here is obviously, is very supportive of this candidate. Thank you for watching this different kind of debate. I don't know what you learned, but to me, the most reliable gauge of who does well on a debate is election betting and I can report after this debate, Biden is down 13%.

Trump, Gavin Newsom, Kamala Harris and Mr. Kennedy are up.

Thank you and Good Night.

Chapter 2

30th ESSENCE Fest

Speakers:

Caroline Wanga - ESSENCE CEO and President

Kamala Harris - US Vice President

Caroline: Um... I'm not going to waste a lot of time because this is about to be a really important conversation. So, what I'm going do is simply invite you to what we here at Essence call, "Chief to Chief". It's a franchise we have where we engage with Black women who are playing chief roles in community, in corporations, and in several other places. And its only intent is to do one thing, it is to tell the story of people who are playing chief roles so that you know the chief within yourself.

And so today, as a part of this series that continues to be an emblem for how great the Black woman is as the CEO of home, culture, and community, we have with us, the first Black female Vice President of the United States, Vice President Kamala Harris.

That's y'all vice president!

Now listen here, we time constrained. I don't need to say nothing else, but ladies and... ladies, gentlemen, community, family... One of the beautiful things about history is once it happens, it can't unhappen.

VP: That's right.

Caroline: And so, what that means is there will never be another day, where we didn't have a Black female Vice President of the United States of America. They can't take that away. But today, I'm going to have a conversation with our Vice President Kamala Harris about the mantle she holds, the seat she has to fill. Every time we have a chief-to-chief conversation, we start with a really simple question, and we ask, "Who is Kamala Harris?"

VP: The Vice President of the United States of America.

Caroline: (Laughing) She said, in case you didn't know. I don't... I can't repeat that.

VP: and... and... I am a wife. I have, we have children, I am a god-mommy, I am an auntie, I am a best friend, I am a good cook...

Caroline: Oh, hold on. Wait, wait, wait, wait... What do you cook?

VP: I cook just about everything. You know today I picked up some Tasso and some Andouille sausage to take back to DC with me.

Caroline: Gumbo with... oh sorry not you weren't inviting them to nothing. Keep going.

VP: And um... and I... I am a fighter for the people.

Caroline: Yeah.

VP: I care about the people...

Caroline: Yeah. Will you do me a favor and just hear a little bit more about why you... why you said that twice? What does that mean to you?

VP: So, I am a child of parents who met when they were active in the Civil Rights movement, marching and fighting for justice. Um... I grew up in a community where it was an extended family of people who told all of us as children, we are young, gifted and Black. That we could do anything, that there was no boundary or border to what we could pursue or believe, and that we have a duty. It's not about that you have the charity, it's about duty, to give back to your community. To know that you've been pulled up and each one must then pull one. And so, living a life of service is something that I was raised to feel a sense of responsibility to do, as do all of us, in various ways. And for me it's in an elective office.

Caroline: And some of that happened in the Bay Area. I mean maybe just a little bit of your life happened over there.

VP: I was... I was born in Oakland, California.

Caroline: Tell them the story of public service coming out of the Bay Area.

VP: I am also a proud HBCU graduate. It must be noted the first HBCU vice president of the United States.

Caroline: Listen, there's HU or something like that...

VP: You know.

Caroline: I was just checking. Don't come for me y'all, but your journey started in the Bay Area in this life of public service?

VP: Yeah.

Caroline: Where does... where does that start for you... you talked about it being important for your parents but like what led you to stay on that path? Because you did quite a few things in California?

VP: Well, there are number of things... Um, I was so, an extended family. My... our second mother, Ms. Regina Shelton, and my Shelton, my... my Louisiana family is here. She was from... They were here earlier...

Caroline: They're not...

VP: There they are. And um... and we... I grew up, we grew up. I lived; we lived on the apartment above Ms. Shelton's nursery school. So, she ran the nursery school.

Caroline: Okay.

VP: And she was part of that flow of folks from the south that moved to California. So, she ran this nursery school, we lived in the apartment on top and she was a matriarch for the community. And we would work at the nursery school, as young... young people. And I would watch Ms. Shelton as she would nurture and advise a young mother. I would watch her as she would counsel young parents on how to get through, when times were rough. And I would see, and I saw in my mother the same type of person, my uncle's, the same type of people. You know I had my uncle Sherman, who was one of the first Black graduates of... of Berkeley Law School, who every time anybody in the community had a problem they'd say, "Call Sherman. Sherman will help you figure that out." And so I was raised by and among a bunch of people who really felt a responsibility to give and to serve...

Caroline: Yeah...

VP: And it was expected of all of us that we would do the same...

Caroline: Yeah.

VP: And that is the life I've chosen to live.

Caroline: So go ahead, because I think many people unders... I... I especially for Black. Right? We live in community and the lawyer in the community is everybody's lawyer.

VP: That's right, for every reason.

Caroline: The store owner is everybody's store owner, whether you got money or not, you get a IOU all those sorts of things and so I think it is very familial, and... and... and... um, selfless to exist in the Black community. When you think about then and... and one of the things we are hearing a lot in this season is about how consequential this election season is. That is a word that's being used a lot but means something different as we look at what this particular season...

VP: Yes.

Caroline: ...will leave us with if it doesn't happen in a way that this community needs to participate to make it happen. Tell us a little bit about what consequential means in this time and why this consequential is very different than any other one we've had in recent history?

VP: Caroline, and everybody here, this is probably the most significant election of our lifetime. You know, we have said it every four years, but this here one, is it. We are looking at an election that will take place in one hundred and twenty-two days...

Caroline: A hundred and twenty-two.

VP: Where on one side, you have the former president, who is running to become president again, who has openly talked about his admiration of dictators and his intentions to be a dictator on day one, who has openly talked about his intention to weaponize the Department of Justice against his political enemies, who has talked about being proud of taking from the women of America a most fundamental right to make decisions about your own body.

And then last week understand, sadly the press has not been covering it as much as they should in proportion to the seriousness of what just happened. When the United States Supreme Court, essentially told this individual who has been convicted of thirty-four felonies, that he will be immune from essentially the activity he has told us he is prepared to engage in if he gets back into the White House.

Understand what we all know in one hundred and twenty-two days; we each have the power to decide what kind of country we want to live in. Understand, what we know, when there has been a full-on intentional attack against hard fought, hard won, freedoms and rights. When I talk about the family that raised me, yes, they took me in a stroller as they were marching for justice knowing that justice will not be achieved unless we are prepared to march and shout and fight for it. And one of the ways we do that is through our vote. This here election, let's think about the significance of the United States Supreme Court. Two years ago, and some days now, we commemorated a decision by the United States Supreme Court, the Dobbs decision, that undid the protections of Roe V. Wade. Understand how that happened, the former president who wants to be president again hand selected three members of the United States Supreme Court with the intention that they would undo the protections of Roe V. Wade and they did as he intended.

The court of Thurgood and RBG took the most fundamental right, the right to make decisions about your own body and on this subject, I think we all believe and know, one does not have to abandon their faith and deeply held beliefs to agree that government should not be telling her what to do with her body. If she chooses, she will talk with her priest or her pastor, her rabbi or her imam, but the government should not be telling her what to do. Understand that the former president who is up for reelection has said he is proud of what has happened. Proud of the fact that our daughters will have fewer rights than their grandmothers, that we have seen in state after state they're passing laws, punishing health care providers in Texas providing for prison for life, for a doctor or nurse who provides reproductive care. Understand laws being passed and proposed that make no exception for rape or incest. Caroline, you asked me about the things that have influenced my career...

Caroline: That's exactly right.

VP: So many of you know I was a prosecutor. You may not know one of the reasons why. When I was in high school, I learned that my best friend was being molested by her step-father. And I... when I learned, I said to her you have to come live with us. I called up my mother, my mother said of course she does, and she came and she lived with us. So, I decided at a young age I wanted to take on what I could do to protect women and children against violence.

The idea that these so-called leaders would be passing laws that make no exception for rape and incest, that are essentially telling a survivor of a crime of violence to their body, a violation of their body that they have no right to make a decision about what happens to their body next. That's immoral. And that's what's happening in our country right now. You look at the taking of fundamental freedoms and rights in Georgia, passed a law to deny people and make it more difficult to have freedom to access to the ballot, passed a law that makes it illegal to essentially give people food and water for standing in line to vote. The hypocrisy abounds, what happened to, "love thy neighbor"? So, look at what they're doing.

Caroline: I want to pick that up.

VP: And all of this is at stake.

Caroline: Yes, so you've been on an economic tour, you've been on a reproductive freedom tour. Somewhere in this audience or on the internet is my niece IO known as Yo-yo to me. And she is somewhere between eight and thirty-two years old and one of the things that happened when you became vice president is IO told me that when she becomes president, her... her platform is going to be ice cream.

VP: Alright.

Caroline: Why do I share that? Because I was excited about IO thinking that she could be president and that ice cream would be the most important issue in the country, because the other stuff ain't a problem no more. As I look at this, the upcoming election, I'm looking at IO and I'm trying to prepare myself to have a conversation with her, that her doctor may not think her health care is important. That she may not be able make a minimum wage to aspire to meet a... a worker occupation that matches her intelligence. I am worried that I have to have a conversation with IO about why her brother Xavier may not be safe and it's a conversation I didn't have to have with my little brother. I am going to be handing off a world that has gone backwards, not a world that just didn't go forward.

VP: Yeah.

Caroline: So, while we've talked about what we know are some of the topics that come from those that aren't looking out for us. How do we make sure the things that are important to our community and again you've been on reproductive freedom, you've been on economic freedom, how do we make sure because we don't all sit on an administration and we don't all know the technicality for the woman that's going home and is taking care of home, family and community. How do I make sure that Caroline doesn't have to have that conversation with IO in a hundred and twenty-two days?

VP: There are many ways, but in one hundred and twenty-two days, it's your vote. I mean, here's the thing about elections and this is maybe the inside deal my... my former colleagues the congressional Black caucus can tell you. The people who make decisions at that level often will pay attention to either who's writing the checks or who votes. That's a cold hard reality. And so, when we vote that is in a democracy as long as we can hold on to it, the power that we have as individuals to weigh in on who is making decisions based on what we value and care about. You know, I'll give you an example of why elections matter, there are many.

Caroline: Yeah.

VP: The issue of Black maternal mortality.

Caroline: Let's talk about that.

VP: So, I have been working on that issue for years with my colleagues from the CBC when I was in the Senate and now as vice president. Why? Because Black women in the United States of America are three to four times more likely to die in connection with childbirth than other women. And we know that there are variety of reasons for that, but we also know that this is a health care crisis of the highest order that has received very little attention proportionate to the seriousness of the matter.

So, I worked with my colleagues when I was in the Senate, we passed a number of bills and when I came into the United States- when I came in as vice president, I continued to work on it and one of the things I found is this, that I was looking at, well for women on Medicaid which states are providing for postpartum care not just for two months but for up to twelve months and I realized when I came in as vice president that only three states would extend Medicaid coverage for post-partum care from two months to twelve months. I... I don't have a problem shaming people sometimes, so I challenged the states to extend it and now forty-six states have extended Medicaid coverage for postpartum care. There is a direct connection between this and Black maternal mortality but here's the other thing back to the other point about freedom of choice, the majority of Black women in America live in the south. You know that in the south we have some of the highest rates of Black maternal mortality, in the south except for the state of Virginia, every state has an abortion ban. And what I find a hypocrisy upon hypocrisy by some of this extremist is the same one saying they're passing these abortion bans because they care about women and children have been completely silent on the issue of Black maternal mortality. So, don't come us, gaslighting us about where you've been and where you haven't been on important issues that relate to... to what we know every day affects our sisters, our mothers, our aunties, our grandmothers, and could affect our daughters.

Caroline: So, if you were... if we were to take that right because I think that part of what we do with this conversation on Chief to Chief is make sure that folks really walk away with the call to action for what's different for them. You talked about this engagement in voting and civically and there are folks in this room that probably have voted and there's folks in this room that maybe haven't voted. But what are they to see from the vote. Go in one hundred twenty-two days and vote but what will be different for them if they do so that those that maybe are considering not doing have a reason to get up that day and do it as well.

VP: So, I'm gonna... what we know is that you can have an idea of what will happen when you look at what has happened. So, I'd ask people in the room to raise your hand if you received student debt relief because you voted in 2020 and Joe Biden and I came in office and were able to forgive billions of dollars of student loan debt. Understanding how it impacts all communities and especially ours. I would ask anyone to... to think and you don't have to tell anybody about this, have you or a family mem... member, suffered from medical debt. We are in the process of saying that no longer can medical debt be counted against a credit score. Right. Because you see, we came in office and we knew because we... we... we are of and care about the people as opposed to the richest billionaires which is who the former president gave a tax cut to and then created one of the largest deficits our country has ever seen. We know medical debt comes about because often, most often, a medical emergency, which nobody invites upon themselves or plans for. And it can result in tens to hundreds of thousands of dollars in expenses that you did not plan for and create debt and then would be used against your credit score. What is your credit... most people know the number of their credit score like you know your weight, especially with all those apps now, right?

Caroline: That was shade...

VP: I just want...

Caroline: That was shade... we gon' talk about that later.

VP: But the credit score makes a decision then about who's eligible for car loan or a small business loan or getting an apartment lease. And what's wrong about medical debt being used in the credit score is the credit score is supposed to be a measure of whether you're responsible with money. A medical emergency is not about that issue. What we have done to cap the cost of insulin at $35.00 a month. Raise your hand if you have a family member who has diabetes. Right. So, and what we know that Black folks are 60% more likely to be diagnosed with diabetes. We cap the cost of insulin $35.00 dollars a month. We have finally allowed Medicare to negotiate drug prices with the big pharmaceutical companies to bring the cost down. So, I say, look at what we've done to know that when you voted in record numbers, people voted in record numbers in 2020, this is what was able to happen and when everyone votes in those numbers again in one hundred and twenty-two days, we can see it through. And seeing it through includes what we intend to do to raise federal minimum wage, what we intend to do to bring down the cost and make affordable childcare a reality for all families, we have said 7% of your income, not more than 7% of your income should have to go for childcare. What we are in the process of doing affordable housing both for renters and those who want to be first time homeowners. We have a plan, we need congress to agree that if you are first... the first generation in your family to seek home ownership you'll get a $25,000.00 tax credit to help you with the down payment.

Caroline: So... so, one of the things that the Essence brands specifically represent is over five decades of a legacy of showing demonstrating and equipping the Black woman with the power and influence she has on all.

VP: That's right.

Caroline: When she turns her head left, the world turns left. When she decides to do something other people decide to do it at a different price than they're paying her to do it- I'm sorry different speech... the value of what she delivers, is not always returned at the value of what somebody who mimics what she did is delivered.

VP: Right?

Caroline: So, for fifty years Essence has been teaching this member of human community called the Black woman that she has a power that just needs to be unleashed versus she doesn't have a power and because she has a power, everybody around her follows her power, which I would then say that those that are here with us live and those that are here with us virtually have the power to make this country be whatever it needs to be for the Black community.

VP: That's right.

Caroline: So, with that being known, whether its's the vice president of the United States or anybody else. Madame Vice President, you are speaking to the most powerful ballot community...

VP: That's right.

Caroline: ... we have. They're the CEOs of home, culture, and community for all. So, if you were to be talking to them about what their power can do for Black, through the lens of the chiefs that they are of their community and you knew that it was what you say that's going to make them do the thing, that's right for them, what do you tell these chiefs about what the need to do with that power in one hundred and twenty-two days?

VP: First, you've already said it, but I will say it to repeat because it bears repeating all the time. We, you, we have extraordinary power, and we can never let anybody take our power from us. Never let anybody take our power from us and never be shy about our power. We must encourage in each other, ambition. Ambition is a good thing. It is good to know one's power and then to go for what you want knowing you can achieve it. That is very important, we do not need to step quietly.

Caroline: We don't know how.

VP: and... but... but and never we and never... and never allow the circumstances or the situation that we know we experience whether it be pay gaps or anything else to make us feel small or alone. I'll say in particular to the younger women who are here. You are on many occasions in your life going to be in a room where you will be the only one who looks like you or has had your life experience, and what I demand of you, is that you always walk in those rooms with your chin up and your shoulders back, knowing everybody here is in that room with you expecting that you will carry the voice that is the strength and power of your voice. I will beseech you; don't you ever hear something can't be done. People in your life will tell you, oh it's not your time, it's not your turn, nobody like you has done it before. One of the things I love is they'll say, oh it's gonna be a lot of hard work... Don't you ever listen to that. I like to say, I eat no for breakfast. I don't hear no. I don't hear no and don't you either.

Caroline: I'm stupid, I'm trying to think what my breakfast word is. I need some time. I don't have one but I'm sure there's one there. Well, so... so as we... as we close this conversation but not this topic, as a person who has responsibility to be guide and guardian of this culture artifact, we call essence, that belongs to our community, there has never been a more urgent time for the CEOs to make the decisions they have the powers to make. There has never been a bigger time for you to believe that you can shift the circumstance of the community that you have not just past survival but to exactly what it should be based on how you contribute and exist. So, I'm asking you, as being a part of that community, to not do anything unearned and do everything to understand, what will happen if in one hundred and twenty-two days you go vote? Because what happens after that, will be a conversation you have to be ready to have.

VP: That's right.

Caroline: Do you know which one you want to have? Ladies and gentlemen, first Black female, Vice President of the United States, Kamala Harris.

Resources

List of Must Read Books and Articles or Content to Watch or Listen To: They all warrant consuming more than once. Some content will be made available on Kindle, Nook, Google Play and Itunes. "We recognize that everyone consumes content in their own way."

Project 2025(Transcript Only ebook) Click here
Black Labor, White Wealth: The Search for Power and Economic Justice By Dr. Claud Anderson
Dirty Little Secrets about Black History, its Heroes and Other Troublemakers By Dr. Claud Anderson
Powernomics: The National Plan to Empower Black America by Dr. Claud Anderson
Dr. Claud Anderson | PowerNomics® Corporation of America, Inc. (Please Support Dr. Anderson by visiting his website and ordering these very crucial reads now.

Interview Transcript (Video, Book and ebook) of Robert Kennedy Jr. on the Breakfast Club https://youtu.be/qHplDa AR_LM?si=-x9EyPtXMpTJTmdk

Interview of Robert Kennedy Jr. on Pierre's Panic Room (Video, Book and ebook) Pierre's Panic Room Podcast - Interview with RFK Jr. | Kennedy24

VP Harris' Economic Plan on Roland Martin Live (Transcript Coming, for Book and ebook) https://x.com/i/broadcasts/ 1mrxmMOzaRqxy

Maafa 21 - Black Genocide in 21st Century America - full documentaryYouTube · Live Action Feb 22, 2018 https://www.youtube.com/watch?v=I6XfU8KVkzI

Malcolm X The March On Washington Was DECEPTIVE (except from Message To The Grassroots) https://youtu.be/8MyFy_57aq0?si=C- dMAPLFsdbBFth9

Resources

The Secret Of Selling The Negro
https://youtu.be/E8PBrhFN35c?si=
   1jZLoyBucY7Mc9sN

RFK JR & Robert Kyosaki in Dallas on my birthday weekend.
https://instagram.com/p/C-Zb7NLgVA3/

Dear Obama Lecture By Ayo Kimathi
https://youtu.be/VZ_X_yqnuGk?si=
   SuHppsL5JRb6wWJb

Genocide Part 1 Lecture By Ayo Kimathi
https://youtu.be/mLkP1UeISns?si=
   mJzxuWtnIYMVrkVU

Dr. Claud Anderson on Immigration
https://youtu.be/gJ_C_4bE5Sc?si=iVl1r8Qq4CtDqILK

Dr. Claud Anderson on Roadblocks To Empowerment
https://youtu.be/qZ7GZq2tfoE?si=EPjvtLQv5m-
   OQ8mw

Dr. Claude Anderson PowerNomics
https://youtu.be/V-01fl8uiqU?si=iydn8UFjxyob4IPk

Dr. Claud Anderson Talks Buying Black, Voting Issues, PowerNomics Plans + More
On The Breakfast Club
https://youtu.be/9b4g1leoWcU?si=rX-
   GYW3khduzpCat

Dr. Claud Anderson Discusses America's Race Based Society, PowerNomics + More
On **The Breakfast Club**
https://youtu.be/fW39KOf_f04?si=
   G1yzEKotPpPBQVlk

"Remember, The Black People's Agenda is committed to sharing the most factual and crucial information with you. If there are any other networks, please share them, as *Roland Martin Unfiltered* is the only Black-owned network I am aware of that provides insights directly from the people who have their boots on the ground in our communities—experts and thought leaders in their

fields. Our focus is solely on truth and facts, not personal preferences.

The real question is: Are they delivering the truth and the facts? The views expressed on this show resonate with the Black community far more than those of major networks like CNN, Fox, and MSNBC. That's not to say you shouldn't watch those networks—I do—but if you want to stay connected and in tune with the issues that truly are for us, by us and atter to us, delivered through the eyes of Black experts and thought leaders with boots on the ground, *Roland Martin Live* provides that content."

"Last Note: It's important to be informed about each candidate's policies, beliefs, and promises in order to make well-informed decisions. We should encourage others to do the same."

— The Black People's Agenda

Follow the The Black People's Agenda on X, Instagram and Facebook

The Black People's Agenda is committed to sharing the most factual and crucial information with you. To stay informed, there are several Black influencers you can follow. While you may not agree with all of them, and some may not see eye to eye with each other, the focus remains on the information they provide.

The real question is: Are they delivering the truth and facts?

Consider tuning into Amanda Seales, Tariq Nasheed on YouTube, Marc Lamont Hill on X, Dr. Umar Johnson, Dr. Boyce Watkins, and Roland Martin, who owns The Black Star Network. If you know of any other networks, please share them. Roland Martin's network, in particular, features multiple guests who provide insights directly from experts and thought leaders with boots on the ground in our communities. The views expressed on his show resonate deeply with the Black community, far more than those of major networks like CNN, Fox, and MSNBC.

That's not to say you shouldn't watch those networks—I do—but if you want to stay connected and in tune with the issues that truly matter to us, delivered through the lens of Black experts and thought leaders, the names above are where to start.

About the Author

Author's Biographies:

• **Donald Trump:** Former President of the United States, known for his polarizing policies and strong influence on conservative politics.

• **Kamala Harris:** Vice President of the United States, with a background in law and progressive social policies.

• **Robert F. Kennedy Jr.:** An American environmental attorney and author known for his advocacy in environmental issues and public health.

• **Joe Biden:** Current President of the United States, with a long career in politics including roles as Vice President and U.S. Senator, known for his focus on economic recovery and healthcare reform.

Follow the The Black People's Agenda on X, Instagram and Facebook.

facebook.com/TheBlackPeoplesAgenda

instagram.com/theblackpeoplesagenda

www.ingramcontent.com/pod-product-compliance
Lightning Source LLC
Chambersburg PA
CBHW020750300326
41914CB00050B/43